ON THE OTHER SIDE

ON THE OTHER SIDE

A Journey Through Soviet Central Asia

Geoffrey Moorhouse

Henry Holt and Company
New York

Library of Congress Cataloging-in-Publication Data
Moorhouse, Geoffrey
On the other side : a journey through Soviet Central Asia / Geoffrey
Moorhouse.—1st American ed.
p. cm.
ISBN 0-8050-1229-X
1. Soviet Central Asia—Description and travel. 2. Moorhouse,
Geoffrey, 1931–   .—Journeys—Soviet Central Asia.   I. Title.
DK854.M66 1991
915.8'404854—dc20   90-45805
CIP

Originally published in Great Britain in 1990 by Hodder and
Stoughton under the title *Apples in the Snow*.
Printed in the United States of America
Recognizing the importance of preserving
the written word, Henry Holt and Company, Inc.,
by policy, prints all of its first editions
on acid-free paper. ⊗
1 3 5 7 9 10 8 6 4 2

CONTENTS

PROLOGUE: Irmos   7

ONE   Upon the Steppe   15

TWO   Along the Silk Route   37

THREE   The Great Retreat   57

FOUR   A Desolation That Was Merv   81

FIVE   The Crescent and the Star   101

SIX   Bukhara   132

SEVEN   Samarkand   153

EIGHT   Zagorsk   171

GLOSSARY   188

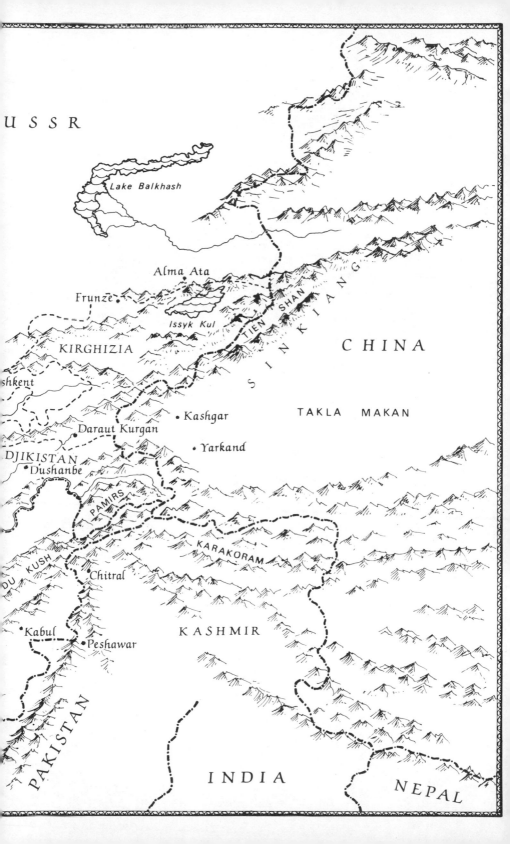

PROLOGUE

The candles in front of the ikonostasis flickered every time the outer door opened and someone was admitted in a gust of keen air. For a moment the drifting fragrance of incense was cut by its sharpness, until warmth rekindled the church and again made it delicately pungent with resin and spice. Other flames swayed in unison whenever a worshipper arrived; in the candlesticks with three branches to represent the Trinity, and in those with two tapers to acknowledge the dual nature of Christ; in the gilded bands of the huge chandelier hanging over the kathedra before the holy door into the sanctuary; and in the little oil lamps mounted under certain ikons on the walls. There was not a dark corner, scarcely a shadow, in the whole building. Everywhere seemed to be full of light; from the flames, from the long clear windows in the outer walls, from the panes of glass in the tower, which rose to the plumpness of an onion dome high above the chandelier.

The light suffused the holy images, which were also everywhere. There were paintings on the ikonostasis, which screened the sanctuary but did not conceal a glowing mural of Christ in Majesty on its farther wall. Another mural faced this at the other end of the church, decorating the arch through which the congregation had entered from the frozen world outside. Smaller ikons hung in frames on every wall, though never so closely that they became oppressively dense. One rested on the proskynetarion, the lectern standing in the nave so that the devout might venerate the ikon closely. It was of the Virgin and Child, who were partly hidden behind an ornate setting of beaten silver. The visible paint lay darkly under a patina of linseed oil that would have been applied to heighten the colours, but had subsequently dulled them as they grew old. The painter was probably a monk, who had created the ikon not as a work of art but as an act of worship; blessing the wood and pigment before he began, preparing himself before taking up his brush, by fasting, by confession, by communion. He would have held himself in ascetic seclusion while he painted; and when he had done, when the wood and the colours had been mingled in this miraculous way, they would have been blessed again and sprinkled with holy water, before being encased in their panel of beaten silver. The image was not sentimental or exultant, like too much religious art in both East and West. Gogol might have had it in mind when he remarked that Russian ikons were dominated by a calm force and were distinguished by an unusual lyricism borne of supreme sobriety.

Yet Russia was far from this place. It took four or five days of hard driving to reach Moscow from here, even when the weather was good, which it wasn't at this time of the year. China was much closer than that. China was only a few miles away, just across those mountains that barricaded the town to the east and to the south.

The church was half full long before the service began, with people preparing themselves methodically for the long convolutions of the Orthodox liturgy. Each newcomer paid some kopeks for the yellow tapers at a little stall beside the door, then advanced towards the ikon he or she wished to illuminate. Unless they were very infirm, they prostrated themselves there, then stood and crossed themselves rapidly and repeatedly three or four times, before reverently holding a new taper to one that already flamed. At the proskynetarion the reverence was completed by bending low and kissing the glass that covered the ikon of the Virgin and Child. Then the newcomers moved to an empty space and stood, as they would remain standing through two full hours, and gazed at the ikonostasis and the sanctuary behind, from which the priests would presently emerge. By the time the bishop himself came through the holy door, coped in gold and with a bulbous gold mitre on his head, the place was packed, though people were still arriving, stamping snow from their feet before entering. A man shuffled in with the aid of a stick, his white moustache dripping moisture onto his breast, where a bright red ribbon and a medal signified the Order of the Great Patriotic War. Another man, more ancient, more fragile but much more alert, followed with dark eyes glancing everywhere as he made his way to the front, head slightly cocked like an old bird listening for worms. A few young people were there, even a number of children, and some worshippers were smartly dressed, with hats and coat collars of fur. But most of the congregation were old women in headscarves, heavy coats and mufflers, legs totally hidden in thick felt boots. Many removed their coats as they reached the warmth of the church and added them to a growing pile on the floor before starting their devotions; and though they became less bulky in their dresses and cardigans, they still looked shapeless, worn-out, used. But not broken. A wizened old crone, who did not appear until the liturgy was half-way through, was so bent that her back was parallel to the floor, but she scuttled like a ferret through the congregation, which parted obediently

9

to let her reach the front. With very few exceptions these were peasants, krestianin, which is virtually the same word as the Russian for Christian. But before they were anything else they were Russians: the people standing shoulder to shoulder in the nave for all this time, and the black-bearded priests moving in and out of the sanctuary at appointed moments in the ritual, and the choir whose singing was almost as important in the sanctity of this place as the holy ikons themselves. There was just one exception to this; just one face that was not European, Russian, Slav. In the choir stood a handsome woman whose features were more rounded, whose profile was flatter, whose eyes were set differently, whose complexion was a shade darker than the rest. It might have been a Chinese face but it was Kazakh, and it belonged here as did no other in that church.

This place was so remote from Russia that, when the Tsar's Cossacks had advanced this far in 1868, they renamed the existing Kazakh settlement Verny, which means reliable. That was because only the most trustworthy troops were sent to garrison this uttermost part of the empire, where dissidents could easily have fomented rebellion without a hint of it reaching the imperial court until it was too late to put down. Verny the town remained until the Bolsheviks took over the historic role of the Tsars and, in 1921, restored the name by which the Kazakhs had known it before the Russians came: Alma-Ata, father of apples. Much fruit had always been grown here.

The singing began after a long reading of scripture by a bald-headed layman, who then took his place in the choir. This was entirely unaccompanied, for the Orthodox have never admitted musical instruments to their worship, but have instead cultivated voices capable of filling any void with irresistibly surging sound: with sopranos who reach transcendent heights that are not attained by brass or reed, and with basses who can make a building tremble as resonantly as any organ (most profoundly, it's said, the basses from Little Russia round Kiev, who have sometimes been capable of supernatural range, occasionally descending two octaves and a fifth below middle C, at which depth the very foundations of a church will stir). To these people, song was as natural as anything in life, so that the Reverend William Coxe, travelling through Russia in the eighteenth century, was taking note of a national propensity when he wrote:

The postillions *sing* from the beginning of a stage to the end; the soldiers *sing* continually during their march; the countrymen *sing* during the most laborious occupations; the public houses re-echo with their carols; and in a still evening I have frequently heard the air vibrate with the notes from the surrounding villages.

So closely had the melodies of the human voice become associated, in particular, with this faith from the moment it reached tenth-century Rus from Constantinople, that the expressions for song and worship have been interchangeable ever since. Just so were the first monks roused for Nocturn and Matins each day: "It's time for singing! It's the hour for prayer!" Even so now, in the Typikon, the manual in which the rituals of Orthodoxy are meticulously codified, all public worship is described as 'singing'.

This was the tradition inherited by the choir, an octet grouped together to one side of the ikonostasis and dressed like the rest of the congregation in everyday clothes. After the long reading they began briefly, with a phrase that would recur, time and time again, until the service closed. *Gospodi pomilui* . . . Lord have mercy: sometimes floating gently, solitary, in the wake of words intoned by a priest, sometimes repeated several times with urgency. Then came longer passages as the irmos, the themes for the day, were developed; in which the sopranos began to skirl to their full height and the basses started to rumble heavily, in a music unlike any other on earth. This was not the florid baroque of Monteverdi, nor was it the measured antiphony of Merbecke, the cool pointing of the Anglicans. It was something far less meretricious than the first and much more animated than the second. It had elements in it of the old Byzantine

11

chants, but its more potent source was the folk songs of the Russian race. It was the sound a people make when their history has been an endless struggle, when they ardently seek relief in divine intervention, and when they are unusually gifted with musical harmony.

The liturgy had been in progress for a full half hour when a bearded student pushed his way through the congregation, taking off his coat as he came. He joined the octet, lent his weight to some of the more complicated chants, and then left as abruptly as he had arrived, when the service was far from done. There were pauses in the singing. One was for a sermon, which clarified some point of theology. Another was for prayers: for the nation and its sacred warriors, for the Patriarch Pimen in Moscow, for the archbishop in Kazakhstan, for peace throughout the world, for Christians everywhere. *Gospodi pomilui, Gospodi pomilui, Gospodi pomilui, Gospodi pomilui* . . . There was communion, in which the people shuffled forward slowly to the rail separating them from the ikonostasis, and the bishop spooned the sacramental elements from the chalice to the mouth of each supplicant. Among these was a young bride in her wedding dress, who had entered the church with her new husband only minutes before, and who left again after receiving the bread and wine, and after doing reverence and lighting tapers at the ikon of the Virgin and Child.

The congregation joined in the singing just once. One of the priests, a tenor with sandy hair down to his shoulders and a voice that rang like a trumpet, turned to the people and conducted them through a choral version of the Lord's Prayer. It was laborious and it began tremulously, and it made its way unsteadily throughout to the final amen; but it was infinitely moving in its very hesitancy, in its wavering, in the sadness of its unfulfilled aspiration. When the last uncertain voice had trailed away the shapeless old women and gnarled old men stood obediently as before, their hands loosely clasped and fidgeting. They went through other motions, crossing themselves feverishly and often, and sometimes bobbing forward from the waist several times in succession, as devout Jews do at the Wailing Wall in Jerusalem. But mostly they just stood and wondered at the drama and the mystery of it all, and listened to the worship of the choir. *Gospodi pomilui, Gospodi pomilui, Gospodi pomilui, Gospodi pomilui* . . .

Here, in the haunting periods of old Church Slavonic, in the long and rolling elegies, in the triumphant crescendos of joy, in the ebb and flow of hope expressed by the high bravura of the soprano and the deep vibrations of the bass, was a people in communion with itself, with its past, with the very ground of its being. I did not see how any Russian, even among those who most despised the fundamental beliefs of the Orthodox, could fail to be stirred to the core by those sounds. One might as well deny one's humanity.

1

Upon the Steppe

The circumstances that had brought me to Central Asia at the beginning of 1989 would have been quite unthinkable even a year or two earlier. Benefactors in Washington, with the connivance of their old adversaries in Moscow, had sent me here. I simply had to submit a report on the geography of the region after travelling through it for a couple of months. I might go wherever I wished, speak to whomsoever I desired, and all doors would be open to me. This was not a trifling collaboration between the once Cold Warriors, even though my own part in it was very small. I was nothing more than yet another expression of glasnost which, by this time, had become so prolific as to have quite lost its novelty, except to me. Here I was in the Soviet Union for only the third time in my life, never before having been granted such licence as this, not even having ventured beyond the Russian heartland during my earlier excursions, when distrust on both sides had been well-nigh absolute, communication extremely limited.

How very different things would be on this journey. Previously I had travelled alone, but now I was provided with a companion, both to reinforce my prentice Russian and to exercise the authority Moscow had vested in the enterprise. Evgeni, in short, was to unlock any doors that didn't instantly swing open at my approach. He had met me when I stepped off the plane from London, his bald dome protected from the freezing air of January by a very wide fur hat, originally his wife's, which made him look uncannily as the late Jawaharlal Nehru might have appeared had his head been jammed into an especially fluffy beige and white powder-puff. He was older than me, but we were near enough contemporaries to have lived through a great deal of the same history, starting with the Second World War, when we had both been children. What a strange cycle of suspicion and amity, alliance and hostility our countries had been through in those fifty years. In the light of some events in that time it was mildly surprising that the pair of us had survived long enough for this liaison to occur.

Evgeni was totally bilingual, though he had never visited the West, let alone any English-speaking part of it. He had acquired his expertise in my language, he said, entirely by reading the classics of our literature and by listening to the World Service of the BBC, surreptitiously for ages but quite openly in the past year or two. His grasp of English grammar was faultless, his vocabulary was impressive, and only a slightly clipped diction and the occasionally eccentric choice of word separated his speech from that of a fluently literate Englishman. On our first evening in Alma-Ata he seized the menu the moment he reached the dinner table, announcing as he did so, with a vigour that made his jowls tremble, "I am *wolfishly* hungry tonight!"

We were quartered in the principal hotel, whose dining-room included a stage and enough floor space for dancing

16

as well as meals. On the stage a four-piece band was warming up as we arrived and almost at once launched into a disco number that would have been utterly unmemorable if it had been played on a solitary and unamplified instrument, or sung without accompaniment, for the tune went nowhere in particular and the words were repetitively banal. But with an electronic organ, a decent drummer and a pair of electric guitars backing the vocalist, 'Apples in the Snow' became curiously attractive, catchy enough to have me humming it to myself in odd moments afterwards. Together with a companion piece, 'White Roses', it seemed to be top of the pops in the Soviet Union, for both were played wherever I went in the next few weeks, pursuing me from one hotel to another throughout the length of Central Asia. The thumping beat of these songs soon gave way to something dreamier that first night, however, for the dining-room was almost wholly populated by the middle-aged and the elderly. Two separate Intourist parties, one of Russians, the other of Poles, filled the place, and the moment the music settled to an appropriate tempo rotund people began hauling partners to their feet. Quite a lot of the couples were deprived-looking matrons stepping the floor together.

"It's a bit sad, isn't it?" I said, nodding in their direction, "to see all those women dancing together without men?"

Evgeni's expression, normally vigilant, with restless eyes that missed nothing, instantly became mournful.

"Of course," he replied. "It's the result of the war, you know."

He meant the Second World War, not the one his country had been fighting for the past decade in Afghanistan. He insisted on this even after I had pointed out a dozen or more husbands, stolidly conversing at the table without their womenfolk, oblivious to the dance just like men of the same age and indifference in England. The Great Patriotic War of 1941–45 had so ravaged this nation that there was a deep need in the Soviet psyche to remind the outsider of its devastating effect, even when there wasn't the slightest connection.

I came across another reminder of the war's place in the mythology next day, when walking through a park. Coming down an avenue of trees, we found our way blocked by a colossal monument in bronze, whose soldiers and other less distinct figures postured heroically, crushingly, from this single huge mass of dark metal. In front of the bronze lay a long slab of polished black marble, from which a flame issued in memoriam. This was to salute a General Panfilov and twenty-eight of his men who had been drafted from Alma-Ata in 1941 to defend Moscow; doing so, according to the inscription, by repulsing fifty German tanks on the outskirts of the capital, for which all had been made Heroes of the Soviet Union. I knew of no British memorial that had a flame burning perpetually, or one that had a permanent guard of honour mounted (day and night, changed every hour, according to Evgeni) by children. Four teenagers stood by, each dressed in the blue greatcoat and winter cap of the Army, each holding a proper-looking gun at the high port. The commander of this little squad, I noticed, was a girl. She it was who stepped briskly forward when a wedding party arrived, and showed the bride where to place her posy of flowers beside the eternal flame.

Her sister in arms was drilling a larger platoon of young communists not far away. Again clad in exact reproduction of the Army's winter uniform, they were practising the slow march, jackboots goose-stepping horizontally, free arms swinging emphatically across the body from right to left, just as the soldiers do when coming to mount guard at the blockhouse containing Lenin's corpse outside the Kremlin. Evgeni and I stood watching for a moment from the middle of the path until the pretty commander brandished her baton and very sternly indicated that we should get out of their way. I could see how, with adolescent girls all over the country presumably in training like this, the Soviet catering industry, such as it was, need never run short of those battleaxes who had invigilated the comings and goings on every floor of every hotel I had ever stayed in here.

We had gone through the park so as to inspect a church

which was said to be one of the two tallest wooden buildings in the world, constructed without even a single nail. It had been turned into a museum during some anti-clerical push, and workmen were filling it with seats for a concert that was to be held that night. Although it had been allowed to deteriorate dustily inside, its pastel outer walls were freshly painted, emphasising its Classical elegance, which was in striking contrast to the domineering heaviness of the war memorial. It had three domes, all set many times with windows, and there was much fenestration at ground level as well. The entire structure seemed to soar from the snow-bound park amid the leafless trees, springing from a sensibility that was evidently more delicate than the one that had created the massive bronze, though in each case the intention had been to glorify.

In the angle formed by two buttresses beside the door there was another difference, contrasting this time with the paramilitary earnestness a few hundred yards away. A young mother stood sheltering from the wind beside a pram. She was tall and slim and she was aquiline, quite expensively dressed, with leather boots covering her legs and a dark sombrero poised levelly on her head. The child was silent and she paid it no attention at all. Nor was she aware of being watched. She was reading a book, quite a thick one, quarto size and well bound; and she was utterly absorbed in its words, turning a page very carefully with her gloved hand just once during the several minutes when I stood and stared. I would have given much to speak to her and to know who it was that captivated her so. But Evgeni was becoming impatient and had started to walk away.

What little elegance there was in Alma-Ata was of the same lineage as the converted church and the cathedral of St Nicholas, in which I attended the liturgy. A number of Russian buildings had survived from pre-Soviet times, from the end of the nineteenth century or the beginning of our own, and even when these were the meanest cottages they still bore the marks of craftsmanship in the carpentry of the window frames, the shutters and the doors. They brightened the streets with their patterns of burnt sienna, eggshell greens and blues, while the icicles dripping from their eaves made them almost artificially picturesque. Otherwise this was a city of relentlessly grandiose public architecture without a trace of charm, and of concrete barrack blocks for the proletariat which were even meaner inside than without; and there they were stultifying enough. Along such streets red trolleybuses hummed efficiently, partly because there wasn't a great deal of other traffic to get in their way. It struck me more than once that this could probably have been any sizeable place anywhere in the Soviet Union. To establish its whereabouts one needed to keep an eye on its citizens, of whom at least as many were obviously Slav as those resembling the Kazakh woman in the cathedral choir. Apart from that, there was a solitary mosque, but this was of indeterminate pedigree. Had it not been for a modest cupola on the roof, with the crescent of Islam perched above, it could have been mistaken for a large bungalow with a verandah rambling round its sides to protect people from a blistering sun. I had seen such buildings many times, far beyond the mountains that hemmed in Alma-Ata to the south, though I had never before seen one used by Muslims for worship. India is the birthplace of the bungalow and, although the word originally meant a Bengali style of house, it eventually spread throughout the subcontinent, largely because the imperial British favoured it.

Those mountains were a spur of the Chinese Tien Shan massif and they rose in a series of ridges and peaks to 15,000 feet, a formidable obstacle at any time of the year and, in winter, totally impassable. The city crouched in their lee, open only to the north, in which direction there was space of such magnitude that it could intimidate the traveller as much as the mountain wall. Alma-Ata was on the very edge of the steppe, the virtually featureless flatlands which went all the way up to the forests of Siberia, though that was as nothing compared with their distance in the other direction, between the Great Wall of China and the Hungarian plain. An attempt had been made some thirty years earlier to cultivate the steppe in northern Kazakhstan in one of those mighty communist endeavours that are intended to rouse patriotism as much as to solve economic problems, and for a little while vast areas were ploughed and cereals were harvested. But then the Virgin Lands programme petered out in the face of natural difficulties as much as anything; a harshly hot or a cruelly cold climate, with nothing much in between and very little rain. It was now a quarter of a century since Moscow had been forced to admit what the Kazakhs had always known: that the steppe is really fit for growing grass and not much else.

The Kazakhs were a nomad people, descended – like the Kirghiz, the Turkmen and the Uzbeks – from Turkic invaders from the north-east, who overran Central Asia in the sixth century.* This was warrior stock, which eventually provided the backbone of the Mongolian army that Genghiz Khan led to conquests on a scale unheard of before his time and scarcely imitated since. The Chinese had their own theory for the origins of these fearsome tribes, believing them to be a branch of the Hsiung-nu, who were traditional adversaries from the mountainous region north of the Gobi desert. According to this mythology the Turks had been wiped out in some obscurely ancient time by an unspecified enemy. The sole survivor was a ten-year-old boy, left to die with his feet cut off but nourished back to health by a she-wolf. Eventually the two had intercourse and, having impregnated the wolf, the boy disappears from the tale. The wolf took refuge in the Tien Shan and there produced a litter of ten males, which she reared to maturity. Each married a human, multiplied and dispersed. One of them founded the line which after several generations became the Turks.

This fable is as serviceable as any that might be concocted, for there is no written record of anything in Central Asia until two centuries after the Turkic invasion is believed to have occurred. The genealogy of the Kazakhs does not

* This Turkic blood did not reach the region we know as modern Turkey until late in the eleventh century.

21

become much less hazy until it is possible to identify them with the Kypchak tribes, a sub-species of Turk who were part of the Mongolian army which marched on Russia early in the thirteenth century and held it in thrall from 1240 to 1480. This was the supremacy of the Golden Horde, which was initially imposed by Genghiz Khan's grandson Batu, whose army besieged Kiev – seat of the Russian grand prince and also of the Orthodox metropolitan – and reduced it to rubble within a few days. The campaign which subjugated the entire country lasted no more than three years, and by then numerous cities had been sacked, their populations slaughtered, the economy wrecked. Many Russian princes fled to Hungary, Galicia and other refuges, but some remained and were allowed to retain their thrones as puppets, provided they showed enough humility; which in the case of Alexander Nevsky (lately triumphant against the Swedes and the Germans along the Baltic and elsewhere in the north) meant a long journey to Sarai, capital of the Golden Horde, and prostration there before the khan. Scholars reckon that the Mongol conquest, not the Bolshevik Revolution or the Second World War, remains the most traumatic event in Russian history, so searing to the national pride that the chroniclers of those 240 years very deliberately obscured the fact that their country had been conquered. They chose their words most carefully to suggest that the Mongol depredations were of no greater significance than earlier raids by rovers from the steppe, and that the heroic defenders had swiftly repaired the damage so that life implicitly went on as before, the moment the marauders had gone. The reality was that, even in the puppet princedoms, the surviving populace was taxed to the bone in order to maintain the administrative machinery imposed by the Mongols, and other crippling forms of tribute were exacted.

It has been said that the most powerful reason for Russian expansion into Central Asia was the bitter folk-memory of that age spent under Mongol domination: that, subconsciously at least, the Russians were getting even for the humiliation they had suffered in their medieval time. Their advance south below the long treeline of the Siberian taiga began early in the eighteenth century, just before Peter the Great's death, but was not completed for over 150 years. It was as much a matter of gradual annexation as of open warfare and in this it bore a striking resemblance to the British conquest of India, which was taking place at approximately the same time. The first objective was to subdue the great blankness of the Stepnoy Kray, the steppe region of the Kazakhs, who roamed its grasslands in nomad parties with their horses and their other herds. The nomads were grouped into clans, and the clans gave their allegiance to one or another of the three Kazakh hordes – no longer the military striking-forces of old (which is what the original Turkic *orda* meant), but each a kind of mobile confederacy. When Abdulkhair, Khan of the Lesser Horde, made his peace with the Russians in 1730 the way was open for further progress into the heart of the steppe, though this was often enough resisted locally by some Kazakhs who thought their khan treacherous, and others to whom any word of his would have meant nothing anyway, their loyalties belonging elsewhere.

By the time the Tsar's writ ran through the Stepnoy Kray, there was an extensive immigration by the Russian peasantry, who had been despatched thither to settlements which would establish a political presence close to China and counter any inclination of the Muslim Kazakhs to rise against their Christian overlords. That is how civilian Slavs came to swell the ranks of the soldiery soon after Alma-Ata was translated into Verny in 1868. Every householder was instructed to plant trees outside his dwelling in order to improve the appearance of the place, as well as to give shelter from the summer heat. There was one other purpose in the patient acquisition of a not particularly attractive immensity of flatlands. The completed annexation of the steppe region made expansion across the rest of Central Asia much easier. By the time those saplings had first blossomed in Verny, two ancient cities of the Uzbeks, Tashkent and Samarkand, had become part of the Russian Empire as well. By 1870 Kirghizia had been annexed, by 1881 there was a

Russian garrison as far to the west as Ashkhabad and, before the nineteenth century was over, the Tadzhik lands had also succumbed. The whole imperial progress, down to the mountainous barriers of the south, had been inevitable from the moment Peter the Great was seized with the notion of a secure passage from Russia to India for the purpose of profitable trade, as that other great imperialist Lord Curzon subsequently recognised. "Russia was as much compelled to go forward" in his opinion "as the earth is to go round the sun."

This wilderness of plain and mountain in the middle of the greatest land mass on earth was not merely so remote that only the most trustworthy officers could be stationed there: it was also so isolated from normal society that it was perfect for imprisonment, as both the Tsars and their communist successors appreciated well. When Dostoievsky had escaped the firing squad for anarchy, his sentence after time in gaol was completed by exile as an army private at Semipalatinsk, on the northern edge of the Stepnoy Kray. When Trotsky fell foul of Stalin he was banished to Alma-Ata for a couple of years before being further deported overseas, where the assassin's ice-pick awaited him in Mexico.

As I ventured with Evgeni out onto the steppe, I discovered other exiles, other places of servitude, much less well known than either of these.

We were driven one day across the wastes to visit a collective farm in cold so intense that, within seconds of stepping out of the vehicle, I could feel the hair in my nostrils beginning to ice up. Mothers towed children and shopping on small sledges, striding briskly to keep their circulations on the move, and a horse waiting patiently between the shafts of a sledge as big as a sideboard kept stamping its feet, one after another, so that the iron-shod hoofs would not freeze to the ground. We had come through an entrance with a red star decorating each of the gates, and then down a drive lined with poplars, to disembark in a little square. This was the heart of the collective, with a department store, a small hotel and the building from which the enterprise was

24

run, a combination of offices and meeting hall on two floors; with, in the lobby downstairs, a large board bearing the portraits of a score or so of people, more Slavs than Kazakhs, but just as many women as men. Each had gained this distinction by achieving work rates above the norm in the past six months. All looked most worthy but not one of them seemed pleased.

Their work was conducted for the most part in a series of long glass sheds that lay some distance behind the buildings round the square, and beyond a range of apartment blocks much like those I had seen in the city. To step inside the sheds was to switch from a temperature well below zero to one of suffocating heat. A couple of women in sleeveless blouses grinned at me as I gasped in the heavy atmosphere and began to unfasten my outer clothes. Men were working in tee-shirts and slacks, like gardeners anywhere at the height of summer. In one shed they were growing roses, tulips and carnations in readiness for Women's Day in March. In another, onions were ready to crop, next to it cucumbers and tomatoes were well on their way. There was even a glasshouse where lemon trees had recently been planted, with a couple of years to go before they would fruit. I made admiring noises to the collective's director, who was showing us round. The fuel bill, I said, must be pretty heavy to maintain these temperatures for six months or more, not to mention much artificial light.

"Yes," he replied. "Much more than it used to be in the old days here."

I inclined my head, questioningly. Evgeni looked enigmatically at the floor.

"When this was Position 26," said the director, studying my face. I still didn't understand. "*Tyurma!*" he exclaimed.

A prison; identified bleakly by a number, so that nobody but the gaolers would know where it was.

Evgeni looked up. "This was the biggest women's prison camp in the USSR," he said, hissing the last sibilants with enough vehemence to send spit from his lips. "In Stalin's time, of course. A terrible, a notorious place. Kalinin's wife

25

was kept here." His Nehru face, normally impassive, was creased with distaste.

Kalininova had been arrested by no less a person than Beria himself and held for seven years, in spite of the fact that her husband was President of the USSR, a popular old Bolshevik but evidently helpless to protect her, hypnotised by Stalin like a rabbit in the glare of a stoat. She was but one among thousands made captive here between the early 1930s and 1954, the year after Stalin died. Almost all were the wives of men who, often for completely obscure reasons, had been executed or sent to the Siberian camps. Many of the women had perished from hunger and cold, for they were quartered in bare barrack blocks made of earth they themselves had cut from the steppe. Having built their prison, they then mostly sewed uniforms for the Army. It was they who had planted the two lines of poplars along the entrance drive.

"What became of the survivors when the camp was closed?"

"Some were sent to Novosibirsk for rehabilitation. Some were joined here by husbands who had been released, and they stayed to turn the place into a state farm. But some had lost husbands, families, everything by then. It was a terrible time, a terrible time."

Evgeni had been translating these details and he looked stricken as he spoke, making fastidious little gestures with his hand.

"Are any still here? Could I talk to them?"

The director shook his head, almost non-committally. I couldn't tell whether the last inmate of Position 26 had moved on, or whether he felt he had already disclosed enough. "But there are plenty of Germans you might like to speak to. That can easily be arranged."

He smiled at my surprise. Germans in Central Asia? Here?

That is how, a little later, Evgeni and I came to be sitting in the kitchen of a fresh-faced old widow whose first name was Irma, in the village nearest the collective. From the outside her home looked like a traditional Russian domik, such as I had admired in Alma-Ata, but it was built a bit differently. There was an extension to the living quarters, in which a cow and a couple of pigs were kept, while the loft had a dirt floor so that a small brood of hens could forage up there. The livestock produced a powerful farmyard smell in the vestibule off the street, but the moment we were on the other side of the door to the kitchen and the rest of the cottage, there wasn't a hint of animals. We might have been sitting with a Bavarian hausfrau obsessed with hygiene and tidiness. Only a couple of wooden ladles, decorated in the Kazakh style and hanging on the wall, hinted that this was Central Asia and not somewhere in Mitteleuropa.

By the time we arrived someone had been busy on the telephone, for the old lady in her dirndl pinafore was not alone. I could hear a babble of German die away when we knocked, and as we entered I could see that two much younger women were there, as well as three elderly men. We were greeted with a confused mixture of *"Zdravst-vuyte!"* and *"Guten tag!"* which gave the game away immediately and caused everyone to laugh. The younger women were Irma's granddaughters, but the three men came from different families in the neighbourhood. The story each had to tell was more or less common to them all.

Irma and one of the men had been born in the Ukraine, she in Odessa, he in Kharkov, while the other two originated further east, along the Volga. All their families had come from Germany in the eighteenth century in response to Peter the Great's invitation to skilled workers from half Europe, when he was trying to invigorate his backward country and galvanise its natives. Most of these migrants had settled along the Volga, especially in scores of villages near the town of Engels , where they became so numerous and so prosperous that eventually they were allowed to proclaim the Volga German republic within the USSR. This was dissolved the moment Hitler's armies attacked in 1941, Stalin further decreeing that every citizen with a trace of German blood must be shipped so far away from that western front that they could not possibly collaborate with the enemy. The principle was perhaps no more than prudent: the British, after all, had sent many citizens with strange-sounding names to the Isle of Man in 1939 until they could be given security clearance, and one blessed consequence of that order was the subsequent formation of the Amadeus Quartet. It was the implementation of Stalin's decree that was so inhuman in the USSR.

Irma and her three brothers, all in their teens, were separated from their parents and found themselves briefly in Soviet-occupied Poland before they were despatched to Kazakhstan. She married another German there, but lost sight of her brothers during the war and only later discovered that two were living in West Germany, the third in East Berlin. In 1986 the West Germans were allowed to cross the Wall for five days, and Irma flew in from Kazakhstan, and they were all together again for the first time in forty years. But not one of them had seen their parents since the day the family was first dispersed. The old lady began to cry very softly when she told me this.

One of the men, Ivan, had travelled east with his mother and sisters in 1941, having no idea of his father's fate. They assume he was caught in crossfire, because the German panzers were entering Rostov on one side as their train was pulling away from the other. At first they were put into a hostel in the north of Kazakhstan, but one day the children were shunted down to Alma-Ata without warning, leaving their mother behind. They heard later that she had contracted pneumonia and died, but their life had not been too hard since.

The oldest person in the room, Alexander, was twenty-nine at the outbreak of war, when the whole of his village was transported to Siberia, to a camp outside Novosibirsk, where he was pressed into service with the Trud Armia, the Labour Army, which sounded to me much like the Todt Organisation of the Nazis. He had been a bookkeeper along the Volga, but now he was forced to work on the land, where he remained until after the war. He then obtained

28

permission to move to Kazakhstan and to take up his old employment, largely through the good offices of his friend Alexei, who completed our displaced German quartet.

Alexei, the man from the Ukraine, whose ancestors had manufactured billiard balls in Saxony until coming to do the same in eighteenth-century Kharkov, had been living in Moscow in 1941 and promptly demonstrated his Soviet allegiance by joining the Red Army, serving first in the Far East and then fighting on the western front. He had passed muster with the recruiting officers only because, the moment war was declared, he shrewdly abandoned his very German surname and adopted his Russian wife's. He not only emerged from the fighting unharmed, but the end of the war found him in Berlin working in the Soviet administration. An administrator he had remained, rising to the management of a collective, and it was from this substantial foothold in Kazakhstan that he was able to pull the strings that brought Alexander out of Siberia.

Although he had been least affected by Stalin's deportations, Alexei spoke more bitterly of them than the rest. Perhaps because he alone had proved his patriotism at the front he felt the insult more keenly than those who had been obliged to suffer the taunts of fellow citizens far behind the firing line.

"We Soviet Germans were patriots," he declared with some heat. "The deportations were a great shock. We were abused."

But it was Irma who had been called 'Fascist!' in the streets. It was Ivan who had more than once been stoned. It was Alexander who told me how difficult it had been to ensure that not one syllable of German passed his lips for years on end. And there were, he estimated, about a million people like them in Kazakhstan still, another million or so elsewhere in the Soviet Union today. Why, there were enough of them to support their own German-language newspaper, *Freundschaft*, published in Alma-Ata each day. But maybe not indefinitely.

"We must now face the fact," he said, "that young Soviet

29

Germans, our grandchildren, don't much speak the language any more." He shrugged and looked rather tired.

The specifically German strain in the complicated culture of this nation had survived remarkably since Peter the Great. But the diaspora half a century ago had been the beginning of the end.

It was another of Stalin's crimes. People, I noticed, spoke very freely of these nowadays, as they most certainly had not on my previous visits to the Soviet Union. In 1969 a friend in Moscow had discussed politics with me only when walking down the middle of deserted streets or across empty parks, when he could be quite sure he wasn't going to be overheard.

The discovery of the Germans was not my only culture shock in Kazakhstan. Evgeni and I had made the acquaintance of Mrs Usmanov, a Kazakh lady of cheerful disposition and formidable energies, most of which she spent on municipal and communist party affairs. She was a prominent member of the city soviet and in this capacity was the person who made arrangements for anything I wanted to see that wasn't accessible to all and sundry. She was very good at it, and not once did she disappoint. I had said that I would like to visit a purely Kazakh community, one that was closer to the nomad soul of this vast republic than Alma-Ata or any other of the cities of Kazakhstan could possibly be. She grinned deliciously when I asked this and said she knew the very place; though, looking anxiously at my face, she said it was far away across the steppe and would mean a long and tiring journey. It sounded perfect to me, and a couple of days later we set off just after dawn.

The temperature was −25°C that morning and, although it was warm enough in the four-track vehicle, Usmanova was swaddled in an expensive-looking fur coat and hat, as if she were off to the theatre rather than the barren countryside. We left the city behind at a junction dominated by the huge squat watchtower of the traffic police, who appeared to be flagging down everything that came their way. Two officers were questioning a truck driver, another was examining papers beside a car, but a fourth merely raised a hand in salute as we went by without slackening speed.

"Party number plates," whispered Evgeni confidentially. The road stretched straight ahead, as unswervingly as if it had been laid down by the Romans, and I was astonished to realise that, as far as I could see into the distance, it appeared to have been completely cleared of snow, a remarkable undertaking in such conditions as these. This dark line of tarmac simply bisected the endless whiteness on either side, though even after driving for half an hour we hadn't seen a single snowplough, or anything else that might have been responsible. In fact, no such equipment was required; nor was the road gritted, as it might have been at home. Much more cleverly, the engineers who built it had raised it sufficiently above the surrounding flatness for the perpetual wind to do the rest by sweeping it clear.

A line of telegraph poles strode across the landscape on roughly the same course as our own, but these simply emphasised the winter desolation of the steppe. Tufts of sedge and other grasses rose above the snow crust, and the monotony was now and then interrupted by the low shape of haystacks, which, in the grey light of that day, took on the semblance of shipping seen from a distance across a bleak sea. Sometimes a reef broke the tedium of the horizon before the flatness continued as before, inevitably, hypnotically. And across this otherwise featureless steppe we roared and bounced in solitude for long periods, with nothing but the telegraph poles and the tarmac to remind us that other human beings had been here ahead of us. In four hours, 350 kilometres, we twice saw tiny settlements from afar, mud or stone-walled habitations huddled together for reassurance in the numbing emptiness. Half a dozen times we overtook, or encountered coming the other way, drably khaki vans with nothing to distinguish one from another except a solitary word stencilled along the flank in Cyrillic, to announce that it was conveying bread or mail.

Twice we saw riders in the snow, an hour or more apart. Each was mounted on a stubby, shaggy horse, whose head was disproportionately large, an animal bred for enduring hardship and not for grace or speed. Each was clad in a quilted coat, and the flaps of his fur cap were tied down to protect his ears from the frost. Each sat in a bucket of a saddle, his thick-booted feet encased in box-like stirrups, with a rifle slung across his back. The first was watching over a flock of sheep, who were nuzzling the snow to get at the grass beneath. He raised a cautious hand in acknowledgment as we drove by, but otherwise sat stock-still. The second never moved a muscle, but stared and stared at us until we were gone. Nearby was a herd of maybe a hundred horses, who turned to face us before grazing the snow again. Between two and four years old, they would soon be slaughtered to provide the dark horseflesh that even in the cities of Kazakhstan was much more common than beef or any other meat; and much more to the local taste. Both the sheep and the horses were guarded by a pack of large and extremely fierce dogs for additional protection against wolves. Without hesitation, each pack rushed snarling and snapping at the four-track with such menace that I shivered involuntarily. I would not have dared to put a foot outside with even one such dog about. Nor would I have cared much to share the rider's loneliness.

In time, the tarmac gave way to a gravel road and it was after travelling along this for several miles that we came to our destination. The village was not very big, though its streets were extremely wide, lined by low concrete terrace homes, leading to a square which contained – it certainly wasn't dominated by – the smallest statue of Lenin I'd ever seen, scarcely life-size, even taking into account its pedestal. He appeared to be giving the thumbs-up to the old men and boys who clumped past in felt boots, and to the smartly-dressed women in furs and leather coats. This wasn't quite what I'd expected so far out in the wild, but I soon discovered the reason for this fashionable display, for which Usmanova had obviously been prepared. Although it had been a while since breakfast, we were led straight from our transport into a large building, through the crowd of people milling round

32

the entrance. Inside, the place was packed so densely that it was standing-room only except for three empty seats on the front row of the auditorium. We had obviously entered the community hall and some entertainment was about to begin. Usmanova looked as pleased as if she had arranged the whole thing herself, as indeed she might have done.

"Make yourself comfortable in the judge's seat," she said. "They have been waiting for us to arrive. Now the beauty contest can begin."

I wasn't quite sure whether I was having my leg pulled or not. Many odd things had come my way in various travels abroad, but nothing before had been nearly as improbable as being asked to judge a Soviet beauty contest in the middle of the Central Asian steppe. The hall full of chattering people had undoubtedly been waiting for us to turn up, and they clapped as we were ushered in. The moment we were seated four musicians came onto the stage, each dressed in high boots, and cloaks identically decorated in the Kazakh style of ogee shapes and curlicues. It was incongruous that, traditionally dressed, they should be playing electric instruments; while, in front of the stage, a shock-headed young man was fiddling with the knobs and switches controlling a large synthesiser-cum-amplifier. This was not a primitive community, for all that it was so very far from the sophistications of city life. An announcer entered behind the musicians, with a trailer microphone, and began addressing the audience with the same brash noise that touts make all over the Western world, when hailing customers off the streets. And then, one by one, the girls appeared.

They were, without exception, very beautiful. Two of them were breathtaking, raven-haired, with delicate features and complexions in which the blood ran warm beneath the honeyed skin. Little of this was visible, for each girl was dressed in a kaftan which exposed nothing below the throat or above the wrist. Each had a little embroidered cap on her head, and everyone's hair was tied in a long pigtail. One by one they appeared to float onstage, announced themselves and where they came from, then floated off again: all, that

33

is, except the two loveliest, who also had a superior grasp of strategy. They added a sentence or two which might have been verse or possibly a party slogan; at any rate, it went down well each time and earned more applause than anyone else had received.

The musicians then began to play, and in turn each girl reappeared and danced for us. I had seen and heard something similar many times south of the Hindu Kush, especially in the country just below the North-West Frontier. This was plangent music that wavered as it rose and fell, and the movements it provoked were tinged with melancholy. The long-sleeved arms flowed, the fingers fluttered delicately, heads tilted demurely, eyes were downcast obediently. It was very oriental, sweetly chaste, and exceedingly well done for the most part. Two girls looked a little uncomfortable to be so publicly displayed and were obviously glad to head for the wings as soon as their music stopped. One poor child left the stage close to tears half-way through her dance, her composure destroyed by a fault in the sound system, which suddenly transmitted a barrage of discordant roars. She got a round of sympathetic applause, but the best performances were hailed with great enthusiasm.

There was then a long pause, in which the musicians picked up their gear and walked offstage, while the shock-headed youth began adjusting his equipment carefully. Usmanova beamed at me like an indulgent aunt who has taken her nephew to the pantomime for a Christmas treat. Evgeni looked as though he was enjoying himself and had probably never seen anything like it in his life.

"Two of them are particularly fine exponents, don't you think?" he said, with his highly developed instinct for avoiding English vernacular.

I agreed: they were also extremely dishy.

The break ended when the lad in charge of the synthesiser threw a switch, and the hall was suddenly deafened with the boom-boom-di-boom of highly amplified Western rave-up noise. One after another again the girls reappeared, now utterly transformed. The chaste traditional garments had been abandoned, and so had the neatly pigtailed hair, together with the demurely obedient manner. Each girl now came onstage with her hair down, her hips swivelling, her feet tapping and every other part of her anatomy throbbing to the racketing syncopations of the disco sound. Some were clad in leather gear, others in jeans, and a couple of these Kazakh shepherdesses had dared to exhibit themselves in see-through shirts, though the effect was less than it might have been because their breasts and much adjacent flesh had been encased in brassières that were about as tantalising as a horse's nosebag. They looked as if they had spent most of the winter studying videos of John Travolta and his supporting cast, so that they might lose themselves in some West Side fantasy.

The most sensational performance came from a girl who had been one of the best traditional dancers, when she had sinuously and instinctively conveyed the deepest orthodoxies of Central Asia. Now she appeared as a mid-Atlantic raver with her hair down, in a leather skirt and a tight bodice, and with long black gloves. She would have been mildly shocking anywhere, as she writhed and thrust her pelvis towards us, stroked herself and licked her parted lips. Here it was dumbfounding; and the audience, which had gone wild at the earlier performances, wolf-whistling the see-through pair, watched with an excitement that became the more electrifying because it was held in check, even as it mounted in response to the climax of her dance, when it erupted into an ecstatic applause that must have rung out far away across the snows.

Usmanova looked beside herself with pleasure as she clapped and clapped, and said, over and over again, "Khorosho! Khorosho! . . . Splendid! Splendid!" For once, Evgeni's command of English failed him and, baring his buck teeth so that he looked less like Mr Nehru and more like a happy rabbit, he simply spluttered and gurgled his own assent. When I awarded the girl the prize I was left in no doubt at all that I was easily the second most popular person in the hall.

Later, as we bounced back the way we had come across the darkness of the steppe, when I wasn't dozing in the rear seat of the four-track I tried to focus on the real significance of what had happened in that remote place. What were those people approving in their wild applause of the alien dancing? Why were they not shocked, and how had the girls dared so much to repudiate all that they had so perfectly endorsed only minutes before? What was everyone, without exception as far as I could tell, rejecting so demonstratively for an hour or so? It was not merely the priggish rigidities of old-style communism.

2

Along the Silk Route

The man crossing the street was quite unlike anyone I had
seen before. His face was weatherbeaten to the colour of
stained oak, and in profile it was so featureless as to be
almost flat. When he turned my way I could see at once
that it was exceedingly broad at the cheekbones, with a
moustache that drooped on either side of the mouth, in that
manner we think of as Chinese mandarin. On his head was
a mass-produced peaked cap, but one much wider than the
Chinese make. He wore a quilted coat gathered in with a
belt, but it was his leather boots that were the strangest of all
his clothes. They were enormously heavy, so cumbersomely
wide right up to his knees that they caused him to walk
with a fisherman's lurch, as though he'd just stepped ashore
after a week or more at sea. Their pointed toes were curled

so extravagantly that the tip of each boot actually faced the heel. In this case the ungainly walk was that of a man more familiar with riding a horse in some wilderness than with stumping the pavement of a city street. I watched him approach a kiosk, which seemed to have nothing to sell. He made gestures to the woman in charge and she produced a packet of cigarettes from under the counter. The man then paid her from a roll of roubles that he had bent down to extract from the top of his boot.

He was from Mongolia, as much of a foreigner in the chief town of Kirghizia as I was myself, and I never did find out why he was there. But his presence was scarcely surprising, for this part of Central Asia had known a traffic in all manner of people since the earliest times of recorded history, and doubtless before. On the road leading into Frunze was a street of old-fashioned domiki inhabited by Dungans, Muslims of Mongol descent who had been harried out of China by its Ch'ing rulers during a religious persecution in the last quarter of the nineteenth century. In another part of town was a deposit of Uighurs, who had migrated from Sinkiang at about the same time, though their ancestors had once been widespread almost everywhere to the west of China's Great Wall.

They were easily the most intriguing people to settle anywhere in this part of the world, a variety of Turk who had dwelt in Outer Mongolia before descending to China in the eighth century. They then embraced Manichaeism, that strange Persian synthesis of teachings by Zoroaster, Buddha and Christ, whose devotees have also included St Augustine and John Stuart Mill: but their even greater distinction was their literacy in a generally illiterate society. The Uighurs became the moneylenders and the scribes to a vast area of the land mass, which meant that they were indispensable to every other breed of nomad people in Central Asia, if these wanted a share in the developing trade there between East and West. Genghiz Khan himself turned to them in the thirteenth century, when he was hammering out his Mongol Empire and lacked the means to administer it effectively from among his own people, who had no alphabet. The Uighur script thus became the official calligraphy of the Pax Mongolica, so that everywhere under the khan's authority knew two languages of government: the local tongue and Uighur. This was much the same prescription applied six hundred years later in India Britannica.

The native Kirghiz, like the Kazakhs dwelling to the north of them, were nomads by instinct, though this way of life had been diminished somewhat over the past generation or so. It was the tradition of these people to regard sheep as the only reliable currency and, as recently as 1939, there was a recognised scale of values throughout Kirghizia, by which it was reckoned that five sheep were worth one ox, two oxen one horse, five horses one wife, and two wives a gun. The heaviest fine that could be imposed under tribal law in these lands was five hundred sheep. Between April and November the nomad families would move with their flocks of sheep and herds of horses from one pasture to another, setting up their dome-shaped yurts in every encampment until the time came to pack up and wander off in search of fresh grass elsewhere; and when the snows came they would retreat to their stone or turf-walled permanent dwellings, where they stayed put until the winter had passed.

Barter was still practised on the steppe and in the mountains of Kirghizia, though less frequently than before; and transhumance had likewise been modified. Where once whole families, even groups of kin, would be on the move with their animals for six or seven months on end, the long-distance shepherding was now more likely to be done by a couple of men with a pack of dogs and a truck containing all the gear they might need until they returned home. I was not travelling at the most likely time to come across a valley dappled with the domes of an encampment, although many years ago the Austrian Gustav Krist had remarked that while he was in the Pamirs, on the southern edge of Kirghizia, "the heaviest storms raged over the aul without a moment's cessation all through January, yet never once was one yurt blown down".

I saw but one yurt during my own journey, and that was standing in someone's backyard as overflow accommodation. There was a wooden door so small that I had to crawl to get inside, but the top of the dome was well above my height. From the slatted framework of the circular wall, clothes had been hung, and so had decorated woollen pouches which contained utensils and other tackle, and a couple of paraffin lamps to provide the only light. There was a carpet covering the floor and a rectangle of tiles on which stood a cast-iron stove, throwing out much heat. The lattice wall-frame, and the strips of willow that rose above it to the apex of the dome, were covered with dark felt, that invention of Central Asia which preceded spinning and weaving, produced quite simply by fluffing out wool, moistening, beating and rolling it repeatedly until the fibres cling matted together; its big deficiency being that it lacks the tensile strength of cloth. The inside of that yurt was warm and comforting, though the felt outside had been covered with plastic sheeting for greater protection. It was home for a young man, his heavily pregnant wife and their tiny child, who lay quietly in a wooden cot that the girl rocked sideways by pushing on a sort of ridgepole running full length above the baby.

Many of the old traditions persisted as they had always done. The horsemen still hunted saiga, a kind of gazelle, with specially trained eagles. These were first introduced to the head of a freshly-killed sheep which was stuck upon a post, its eye-sockets stuffed with red meat so that the bird would learn to go for the eyes first of all. They still played the game, common throughout Central Asia under various names and said to have originated in Mongol training for cavalry warfare, in which the decapitated body of a sheep or goat is struggled for by a score or more of competing riders, who gallop and jostle until a winner manages to deposit the carcass in some appointed place, which may be miles across rough terrain. As primitive as anything was a

40

habit of some shepherds in response to human vanity. Many of the flocks in Kirghizia consisted of the Karakul breed, whose lambs have that tightly-curled fleece Westerners think of as astrakhan. The younger the lamb the tighter the curl, and I had heard that not only were some lambs killed when only two or three days old, but that the bellies of some ewes were slit open a week before they were due to give birth, so as to get at the even more desirable pelt that lay inside. One day I found myself sitting next to the director of an institute of research in sheep husbandry, and I asked him whether this barbaric practice still went on. Oh yes, he said, it did, and the fleece was very expensive as a result, destined "for film stars and the like" after being auctioned at the big international sales up in Leningrad. Then he leaned towards me with a gleam of amusement in his eye. "But it's not very warm wool, I'm afraid. Just pretty." He giggled at the thought of the excessively wealthy catching cold.

It was nomad peoples such as these who first introduced the utterly different cultures of East and West to each other, and never for one moment could I forget this when most of my journey through Central Asia took me along the line of the old Silk Route. The phrase may be a touch less romantic than the one coined in the nineteenth century by Baron Ferdinand von Richthofen – uncle to the German air ace Manfred von Richthofen, the Red Baron of the First World War – but the "Silk Road" implies that there was a single highway stretching from the Mediterranean to the heart of China, when this was far from the case. A little to the east of Kirghizia, for example, there were three different courses that could be taken to reach the same destination, all of them separated by considerable distances and natural obstacles. One skirted the shores of the Issyk Kul and held firmly to the northern side of the Tien Shan; another passed through Kashgar and continued below the southern edge of that mountain range but above the dreaded Taklamakan desert; while the third curved south from Kashgar through Yarkand and Khotan along the far side of the sand sea. There

41

were other variations elsewhere; and there were also tracks lying roughly at right angles to the main passage between east and west, notably one that came up from India to join the major caravan route at Bactra, which is now Balkh in Afghanistan.

For at least a couple of thousand years before Christ trade in some shape or form had proceeded along many of these tracks, though the full Silk Route was not open before 100 BC or thereabouts. For many centuries afterwards, however, it was the most vital as well as the most legendary channel of communication on earth, not only a conduit for commerce between the known world's extremities, but also the way in which ideas and discoveries were transmitted from one civilisation to another. The Chinese relinquished the secrets of papermaking and of unravelling a silk moth's cocoon into a single unbroken thread, as well as the matter of growing roses, camellias, oranges, peaches and pears. Europe divulged the art of making coloured glass, the cultivation of grapes, cucumbers and figs. From Central Asia everyone else was introduced to the Bactrian camel with two humps and, more importantly, to the horse; also to the art of riding it while at the same time firing an arrow accurately from a bow.

The Silk Route's other historic role was to provoke warfare and invite conquest, from armies which marched and rode along it in pursuit of the booty which they had heard was accessible to a determined invading force. Conquest was eventually to be its death. Genghiz Khan's advance westwards at the start of the thirteenth century prevented the old entrepreneurs from using it as before; and by the time it was available to them again under the Pax Mongolica they no longer needed it, having discovered ways of trading by sea that took a little longer than by the overland route, but were cheaper in the end because they cut out all the middlemen.

There were many of these along the 5,000 or so miles of the main route from east to west, because no trader ever travelled the whole way. A Chinese merchant might set out

with his bales of silk from the walled city of Ch'ang-an* –
the eastern terminus – but at some stage he would exchange
these for coloured glassware or Roman bullion or even
copper, lead or tin, without ever meeting his counterpart,
who had started overland from the Mediterranean ports of
Antioch or Tyre, or from Byzantium itself; and the first
intermediary would probably do business with a second, a
thousand miles further on, at which point there would be
another bartering, to be succeeded by a third, perhaps a
fourth and a fifth, before the silk – its value now much
inflated above the original price – was finally laid before
potential customers in Rome or some other distantly sophisticated place.

There were other hazards, even more to be avoided than
the percentages of nomad middlemen. From beginning to
end the Silk Route traversed very rough country indeed, and
long stretches of it could be lethal for caravans if the weather
turned bad. The seventh-century Buddhist pilgrim Hsuan-
tsang, travelling through the Tien Shan with a party which
lost fourteen people from exposure and avalanche, heard of
a disaster in the same region which almost defies belief: a
caravan overtaken by a blizzard so appalling that every one
of its several thousand human beings and camels was frozen
to death. Apart from natural dangers the traders also had to
contend with brigands and others who preyed on strangers
travelling across their territory.

Of these quite the most fearsome for two hundred years
were the Assassins, who were so deadly that they intimi-
dated every ruler from the Mediterranean up to the edge of
the steppe. They were a Persian sect from the Shiite branch
of Islam, whose activities began towards the end of the
eleventh century when one Hasan i Sabah, a missionary
with some success in converting atheists and Sunni Muslims alike, killed a Sunni muezzin who resisted his
proselytising. He and his followers then seized a number of

* Ch'ang-an was close to Xi'an, where the entombed terra-cotta army
was found in 1974.

castles in the mountains below the Caspian Sea, one of which, Alamut, to the north of modern Teheran, became the headquarters of Hasan, the first Grand Master of the Assassins, and his successors. There, too, was the garden in which the drug *cannabis indica* was grown, to be incorporated into the rituals of those disciples pledged to kill anyone nominated by the Master; from which they acquired their name, hashishins, this becoming slurred into the familiar and terrible epithet. Driven in the first place by religious mania, the Assassins quickly became a byword for political malevolence and treachery, even among themselves. One of their number, a Syrian named Rashid ad Din, once ingratiated himself so skilfully with the Grand Master that only moments before he was murdered did the victim realise Rashid had been nominated to succeed him. Their reign of terror ended only in the thirteenth century when Genghiz Khan's grandson Hulegu besieged the Assassin fortresses and slew every inhabitant on taking them. After which the Ismaili sect, which had fathered this murderous offspring, recovered its reputation for a peaceful profession of Islam, as it has continued to do in modern times, under the leadership of the Aga Khans.

At regular intervals throughout its length the Silk Route offered shelter from the elements and from pillage in the shape of that ancient forerunner of the motel, the caravan-serai. The best remaining example we came across lay on level ground a few hundred yards from the huge earthworks of a fortress which had originally been built in the fourth century BC. From the topmost ridge of these embankments the view of the mountains a few miles away would have been sensational on a clear day, but they were totally hidden by a steadily falling curtain of snow. All that otherwise survived of military engineering was the gatehouse, with a single tower like a stumpy minaret on each side of it. This had been built in the seventeenth century. The nearby civilian architecture was much more rewarding, and was in the process of being restored after various dilapidations. The oldest building was the Islamic mausoleum containing the grave of a fifteenth-century maulana beneath its dome; the most complete a madrassa, a school of religious studies built two hundred years later, with a courtyard surrounded by cubicles, in each of which a young man and his tutor would together have pored over, memorised and interpreted scripture.

Alongside the madrassa, separated from it by only a few yards, was what remained of the caravanserai. None of its brick walls, all recently repointed with mortar, was more than chest-high, though when this was a going concern they would have risen to one full storey and might have been topped by a series of shallow domes around the central courtyard. The internal walls simply created a series of compartments running round all four sides of the building, each about five yards deep. In other words, this was a relatively small caravanserai of sixty rooms, where traders and drovers would rest with their merchandise until they were ready to continue along the Silk Route. The camels would have been brought through the solitary opening in the walls, would have been unloaded in the yard, then led away to graze the surrounding land under the watchful eye of a lad who was travelling with the party for just such a purpose. With a fortress just across the way there would have been little need for these travellers to worry about attack, though some caravanserais were built in vulnerable isolation for no other reason than the fact that the wilderness provided a spring of water, or a mountain stream, close by.

Behind this complex of buildings a village sprawled; and right beside the fortress earthworks, across the highway from the caravanserai, stood that other stand-by of the traveller ever since people and animals began humping goods about, a chai-khana, the Central Asian equivalent of a transport café. This tea-house could not have been there for more than a year or two, but it had been fashioned in faithful imitation of the traditional style, with a series of very low tables at which each customer squatted cross-legged upon a padded bench. In one corner of the room, piled high against the wall, was a stack of multi-coloured quilts. The clientele when we went in consisted wholly of the hard men of the road: stocky fellows in shaggy fur caps and heavy coats who looked quite brigandish themselves, as they slurped up a greasy mutton and noodle soup, which they ate with thick discs of doughy bread. Most were bearded or moustached and heavily unshaven, but one had recently taken a razor to the whole of his face. In front of him were a large number of hard-boiled eggs, and these he was methodically cracking, peeling and eating almost whole, while he kept up a conversation across the plastic table-top with three companions. Sitting opposite me, the only man in the place who had removed his headgear on entering, Evgeni obsessively cleaned his spoon on a paper napkin before eating, and peered suspiciously at the bowl containing his soup. His Muscovite gaberdine was even more incongruous in that gathering than my anorak, yet no one gave either of us a second glance after we had walked in and settled down.

It occurred to me that this warm and steamy place, with its noise of gossip and argument accompanied by the animal sounds of food being hungrily consumed, was in the direct line of a succession which may have stretched back, if not a full six thousand years, to times well before the Christian era. Certainly Alexander the Great had passed this way when he was marching on India in 328 BC for the epic confrontation with King Porus and his elephants at the battle to cross the Jhelum. This was a terminal engagement in some ways because, shortly thereafter, Alexander's troops indicated that they had had enough of his obsessive campaign to reach and conquer the ends of the earth; a mutiny which caused him to turn and begin the long trek home to the Levant.

Alexander's was but one of many names that had rung round here at intervals. As intriguing as any of them was that of Prester John, the Christian king of medieval mythology, whose home was supposed to have been in those mountains behind the caravanserai, now hidden by the pall of snow.

46

That, at least, was the belief of the Crusaders as they fought the Turks at the Mediterranean end of the Silk Route and hoped for assistance from this direction. In reality the prince they had heard of was Gur Khan, leader of the Kara Khitai, a Mongol tribe which had adopted Buddhism and, from its strongholds here in the highlands between Issyk Kul and Kashgar, had driven the Turks so far to the west that Bukhara and Samarkand were taken, their mosques converted into temples for several decades of the twelfth century.

The hearsay that had increasingly fascinated me concerned an ancient meeting place of caravans somewhere along this stretch of the Silk Route. This was first reported by a Macedonian trader named Maes Titianus, and was written down by one Marinus of Tyre, whose account was subsequently incorporated by the Greek Ptolemy midway through the second century in *Geography*, his massive and authoritative study of the known world. According to Ptolemy, Maes Titianus had not himself travelled in the region but had collated all the information possible on the Silk Route by listening to what his agents in the field had to tell. They had mentioned the existence of a Stone Tower, where caravans coming from China would exchange silk and subsidiary goods – in this case apparently spices, ink and steel – for the gold and silver that Rome had to offer. It must have been a scene of enormous activity even if no community of any size was attached to this legendary entrepôt, as was evidently the case. Some details of the surrounding landscape had been passed on by Maes Titianus's agents, who made it sound a pretty godforsaken place, but the only other clues to its location were ambiguous in the extreme. Marinus, himself twice removed from field work on the topic, reckoned that it took the Chinese seven months to reach the Stone Tower and then to return to their base at Ch'ang-an; from which he calculated a distance of 36,200 stades, or 4,140 miles, compared with a distance of 26,280 stades, or 3,020 miles, for caravans coming in the opposite direction from the River Euphrates. Historians and geographers who, ever since, had been trying to identify the

47

place where the Stone Tower had been built, struggled on in the knowledge that these figures could not be relied upon for accuracy. It was well known that travellers at this time, about AD 120, were apt to overestimate distances generously, perhaps because it made a better tale to relay later to the stay-at-homes.

The problem was further complicated by the fact that, in Turkic, Stone Tower translates as Tashkurgan; and in the great wedge of Central Asia that formed the target area there were no fewer than four Tashkurgans to consider as alternative possibilities. One, on the River Yarkand, was known to be a halting place for caravans traversing three different routes, from Kashgar, from Bactra, and from India by way of the Indus Valley. Another was in Uzbekistan, a little to the south of Samarkand. A third was on the River Khulm in Afghanistan. The fourth was in Kirghizia, not far from the present boundary with China. Whichever was the Stone Tower that had seized Ptolemy's imagination, it had to conform with his information that, from Bactria

northward up the ascent of the hill country of the Comedi, and then inclining somewhat south through the hill country itself as far as the gorge in which the plains terminate . . . This Stone Tower stands in the way of those who ascend the gorge, and from it the mountains extend eastward to join the chain of Imaus . . .

The chain of Imaus was the Pamirs, running north from India.

It was the Hungarian-born and naturalised British archaeologist and explorer Mark Aurel Stein who arrived at a conclusion that, since he published it in 1933, has been generally accepted as the likeliest location of the Stone Tower. Any description of Stein himself ought, in the interests of veracity, to add that he was one of the most ruthless pillagers the Western world has ever let loose, in the name of scholarship, on the East. Even the bland pages of the *Dictionary of National Biography* admit that, during

48

each of his several expeditions into Central Asia "he brought back to India and England many hundreds of cases of valuable objects." His most dramatic act of plunder was to extract, by bribing an unsophisticated monk, no fewer than 500 works of art, 3,000 rolls of printed material and 6,000 other documents from the Caves of a Thousand Buddhas, a holy place near Tunhuang on the edge of the Gobi desert. The greatest single item in this haul, the Diamond Sutra of AD 868, the world's oldest printed book of proven date, may be inspected still in the British Museum; illustrations and calligraphy in black ink on a long scroll of greying paper, so that the effect is of rather inferior newsprint.

Stein was persuaded that the mythical Stone Tower was in Kirghizia. Everything in his view pointed to it: topography, climate, local wherewithal. The site obviously had to be in some place where caravans could meet, where camels could graze while the merchants discussed the exchange of their goods. It also had to be somewhere along the Silk Route's main axis, not on one of its tributaries. He believed he had found what he was looking for along the Karateghin valley, which breaches the great natural barrier of the Pamirs and runs from east to west, with the Alayskiy Khrebet range forming its northern side. When Stein was investigating he found the way was wide and easy from the moment the westward road out of Kashgar reached the saddle of the Pamirs, and continued thus for another twenty miles to the Russian frontier post of Irkeshtam, which is now known as Sary Tash, though it has had no official function since the frontier with China was closed in 1960. The valley then continued for another seventy miles to the Kirghiz settlement of Daraut-Kurgan, in a climate less harsh than anywhere in the surrounding mountains, with good and plentiful grazing as a result. At intervals along this valley Stein found traces of roughly-built stone dwellings, but in the end his attention was fixed on a spot about three miles west of Daraut-Kurgan. Here, he wrote, was the village of Chat:

with a large well-cultivated area and a ruined circumvallation of some size occupied during the troubled times preceding the Russian annexation of Turkestan. It is a point well suited for a large roadside station, and it is in this vicinity that we may safely locate the famous Stone Tower . . .

I very badly wanted to see this tumbledown rampart, for the story of the Stone Tower had gripped my imagination ever since I first heard of it at school. From the moment plans had been laid for my journey, I had considered a venture into the remote Karateghin valley to be a high priority, although nothing was ever formally arranged. When Evgeni and I first met and I mentioned this, it was obvious that he'd never heard of the Stone Tower and never been within a thousand miles of it. At once, however, he had been scornful of my idea.

"But that's impossible," he said, with an air of authority. "At this time of the year places like that are quite inaccessible."

In his frame of mind, I thought to myself, he probably took the view that even the woods round Moscow were quite inaccessible. In Alma-Ata and again in Frunze I had asked him to canvass local opinion about the feasibility of reaching Daraut-Kurgan, and each time he reported with great satisfaction that the local experts had fully confirmed his own view that, except in the brief summer, travel in the Pamirs was absolutely out of the question.

"Does that mean," I asked, "that the caravans only moved along the Silk Route up there for a couple of months each year?"

He made a testy gesture which implied that what happened so very long ago was of no concern to him, and that I was beginning to waste his time.

"And do you suppose," I persisted, "that the people of Daraut-Kurgan, the people in Sary Tash, are completely cut off from the rest of the country except for the few weeks after the snow has melted and before it starts to fall again?"

He frowned and shrugged irritably.

He was not, in fact, being deliberately obstructive; and when I asked others about my chances of fulfilling this small ambition, I was given more or less the same response. Not one of them had ever been anywhere near Daraut-Kurgan, but all were convinced that the thing couldn't be done. It mattered not to them that, as I pointed out on my map, a road ran up the valley, that it looked like several routes Evgeni and I had already travelled without difficulty, and that as well as being one of the Soviet Union's chief highways into China – whenever the frontier might be opened again – the road clearly connected with others networking the adjacent Soviet republics of Kirghizia and Tadzhikistan. In spite of such circumstantial evidence that an excursion to the remains of the Stone Tower might be feasible even in January, they would have none of it.

I had already noticed a tendency among people here, whenever the unexpected and unplanned cropped up, whenever the slightly unusual was asked, to think of reasons why the thing could not be done. It seemed to me that this response had become so highly developed over such a long time that it had now reached the stage of pure instinct. It was the very opposite of a normal American response to similar circumstances, which would have been to see what could be done, to try to make the thing work, to give it their best shot; the 'Let's go!' approach to life. I told Evgeni this one day. The people of the Soviet Union and the United States, I said, seen from a position somewhere between the pair of them, had much more in common than either might suppose or would care to acknowledge. But in this respect they were utterly different; and I knew which approach appealed to me the more.

He looked uncomfortable, so I didn't add what I also had in mind. That Mikhail Gorbachev's biggest difficulty in trying to transform the mess he had inherited from Brezhnev and his other predecessors was not nationalism in the Baltic and Caucasian republics, was not settling honourably the war in Afghanistan, was not even raising the economy

51

above the dismal standards of the Third World. The biggest problem of all was how to galvanise every citizen out of a stupefying inertia; as Mr Gorbachev well understood. At intervals along the main roads we passed large hoardings which announced that 'You Should Begin Perestroika With Your Own Self.' They had become almost (but not quite) as common as much older notices, which usually appeared above factory gates, or broke the roofline of an office or a housing block: 'Glory to the Communist Party of the USSR!'

I nagged away so tediously at this contentious matter that eventually Evgeni made a concession. We would find a driver and a vehicle to make an assault on one of the mountain roads leading in the general direction of the Stone Tower; but the moment we found the road impassable we would turn back and there would be an end of it; there would be no more attempts. It was the best deal I was going to get in only the fourth year of perestroika. I sighed and signified my assent; and wished I hadn't next morning when the vehicle turned out to be an ordinary car with almost bald tyres. I was told that nothing better than this was available, that I must take it or leave it; so I sighed again and got in, grumbling. I wouldn't have much cared to use this contraption during winter in the modest hill country where I live, let alone in an ascent to the Pamirs.

For a couple of hours we drove towards the mountains along completely clear roads but, shortly after we began to climb, the snowploughing had stopped. There had been plenty of traffic, however, which had packed down the snow into a perfectly good surface for motoring, provided the driver observed all the usual winter rules. On bald tyres, our man was breaking one of the most fundamental, and we slithered several times when coming round bends. But we made steady progress along the shoulder of a great snowfield, which almost overhung the road on one side and dropped sheer away on the other. We came along the edge of a ravine, where trees concealed a village until we rounded a bend just before the first house, and here the driver stopped to ask about conditions further on. There was scarcely a cloud in the sky, and a brilliant sun threw black shadows on the dazzling snow. The driver went into a house, then reappeared, beckoning us to join him.

A bucket of water hung from a long hook on the verandah, with a thickness of ice on top. It was appreciably colder than it had been down below but, inside, the cottage was made snug by a stove which was burning dried cow dung, that ubiquitous fuel of the peasant all over the poverty-stricken world. The moment Evgeni and I entered, a bulky woman in middle age, dressed in the fashion of relatively emancipated Muslim countrywomen almost everywhere – that is, in pantaloons and long dress, with a shawl covering the head and neck but not the face – put bolsters and quilts on the floor for us to recline on, then began to bustle in with food; the same rounded bread we had eaten in the chai-khana, supplemented this time with a cream cheese and some dried fruits. Three small children crept in and peered curiously at the strangers while their father, a young man, conversed with us. The woman was his mother, not theirs. Islam's proprieties were being observed all the way from the instant hospitality to the seclusion of the wife.

And yet while all this was going on a television set, perched on top of a chest of drawers, the room's only furniture, continued to flicker and fluctuate, its colours clashing with a gaudy floral paper decorating the walls. It was showing part of a serial drama I had already become acquainted with, a German and Hungarian co-production about the life of Bach. At six thousand feet, just below the roof of the world, I was seeking directions from a Kirghiz shepherd to the muted strains of Brandenburg No. 5. The Silk Route was maintaining its ancient role as a channel wherein the cultures of the East and West mingled yet remained obstinately strange.

I wondered later whether I had been made the victim of a careful set-up. The trouble was that I could not speak directly to the shepherd, who knew only Kirghiz and had even less Russian than me. But by way of the driver and

53

Evgeni I was informed that although the road continued for some distance into the mountains as navigably as we had found it so far, a village ten kilometres further on was cut off and would remain so until the winter was over. How, then, did they manage, I enquired? They stockpiled food, enough to last for many months, especially nuts and dried fruits, a diet which was responsible for the remarkable longevity of people round here. Why, our hostess here was sixty-four (she certainly didn't look it) and only six months before had buried her husband of eighty-six, while her mother had lived to 101, but if I thought *that* was impressive then I should consider our host's grandfather, who was yet alive at 110, and capable of carrying 40 kilos on his shoulders still . . .

I did not ask to meet this herculean antiquity and I have regretted it ever since. But I wanted to get on. I was not yet convinced that the Stone Tower was inaccessible.

"So what happens in this village, cut off for the next three months up there, if there's a big emergency, a matter of life and death?"

"Why then, of course, they would use the radio telephone to summon the flying doctor."

"So helicopters go to these isolated places in the mountains? They have landing pads there?"

"But of course," said Evgeni, in a tone that was loaded with what-did-I-take-them-for.

I knew, even as I was about to say it, that I ought not to, that it would be presuming too much on our relationship, because it involved national pride at the most sensitive level. It was needlessly provocative. I said it nevertheless.

"Then let's hire a helicopter, Evgeni. I could do that in the United States. Even in Britain."

"But this is the Soviet Union and you cannot do such things here. It is quite impossible, asking too much." His jowls swung like dewlaps with the passion of the insulted patriot, though he sounded much less like a wounded Russian than a particularly plummy Englishman.

I let the matter drop. It was going to be a chilly ride back. I was fuming with my own resentments that evening, otherwise I would not have allowed the abysmal service in the hotel to madden me as it did. It was not unusually bad, no worse than the norm, one of the things that had not changed a scrap since I first visited the Soviet Union twenty years before. We had gone down to eat half-way through the advertised dining hours, by which time, we reasoned, the Intourist mobs from East Germany and Poland would be near enough the end of their meal to have taken the weight off the kitchen. In fact, the restaurant was deserted when we arrived, most of its lights dimmed. After we sat down the occasional surprised, incredulous face looked round the kitchen door to behold the phenomenon of two men obviously expecting to be fed at this hour. It was fifteen minutes before one of the waitresses approached, and then only to announce that she would go and find out what food, if any, might be available. Ten minutes later she returned to say that we could have some cold mutton and stew left over from the mass production that had been arranged for Intourist, but that would be it. A bottle of wine? Impossible: they'd finished it all last night.

At that point I exploded, very rudely, in English. The girl gave me a look which unmistakably meant that if I was going to be like that there wouldn't even be cold mutton. Evgeni flapped his hands anxiously and told me he would go to see what he could find for himself. He returned a few minutes later hugging a bottle of champagne obtained from the bar downstairs. If anything this made me even crosser, for it confirmed my original suspicion that the dining-room staff had merely been too idle to go and fetch wine themselves. Half a dozen, of both sexes, had now fallen in around the doorways leading from the kitchen to observe with blank curiosity the irascible foreigner who was giving Olga such a bad time. They were not, naturally, going to lift a finger to help her, or us.

I apologised to Evgeni for embarrassing him in front of the girl, but added that it needed more explosions like mine from every single customer before a dump like this even began to get its act together.

"How on earth," I went on remorselessly, "how on earth did you people ever get a man on the moon, when you can't even organise a doss-house down here? What's the matter with this country, Evgeni?"

His answer I shall never forget. He was not petulant, as he had been when I insulted him in the hill village earlier. He did not look hurt, as he could when I was tart about some inconvenience or other; which often happened. He showed no anger to the guest who in such ways too often forgot elementary good manners in the presence of his hosts. Instead, Evgeni leaned back in his chair and said, with the air of someone arriving at a careful conclusion after long consideration, "You see, the basic trouble is this. For seventy years or so everyone has been taught that 'the benefit of the people' is paramount, whereas the benefit of the individual is . . . "

And he spat; viciously, deliberately, wetly; so that the spittle landed on the very spot where the disobliging waitress had stood.

3

The Great Retreat

From my room on the sixth floor I had an excellent view of
the mountains to the south. It was like looking at a long
white wall of such a rough texture that some of its surfaces
gleamed in the late afternoon sun, while others were darkly
hidden in the shadow cast by the bumps across the hollows
in between. The wall was perhaps ten miles away at its
nearest point, but it stretched unimaginable distances in
every other direction, becoming higher and more spectacular towards China, where it rose to pinnacles and ridges that
were thrilling and intimidating in their starkness. These
were the Pamirs, the so-called roof of the world, beyond
which other mighty ranges cascaded in a terrible wilderness
of snow and ice and storm. Well out of sight behind the wall
to the south rose the jagged ellipse of the Hindu Kush, which

I was more familiar with. Some years earlier I had explored its further side, which had been the old North-West Frontier of British India and now separated Pakistan from Afghanistan. I have known nowhere lovelier than the valleys of Chitral leading up to that tremendous boundary, and few wild places that have been more laden with history. There was a sense of completeness in now overlooking one of the earth's great natural frontiers from the other side of the hill.

My view of the mountains was unimpeded, for Dushanbe was a very flat city, smothered in trees which were now bare. Only one or two housing blocks rose above the topmost branches, and then not very far; because, I reasoned, Tadzhikistan was prone to earthquakes so that prudence dictated strict limits on heights. Other than these there was nothing but a tall crane standing idle over some new construction site; and what I took to be the control tower of the municipal airport, because of its shape and because a plane had just landed alongside. It was odd, I reflected, that there should be so much traffic on a Sunday, which was generally made the excuse for inactivity even in this officially irreligious state. That was the third aircraft to land within the past few minutes, which seemed excessive in such an out-of-the-way place, even if this was a city of half a million or so. I shaded my eyes from the declining sun and looked out to the south-west; and felt something jump inside. There was a whole file of planes approaching Dushanbe now; four, five, six of them that I could see drifting out of the sky in line ahead from the direction of Afghanistan.

I suddenly realised that I was witnessing one of the biggest retreats in the history of warfare.

We were into the first week of February, and the Soviet Union had undertaken to withdraw its troops from Afghanistan before the month was half-way through. According to the World Service of the BBC, which I listened to on my transistor almost daily, the withdrawal appeared to be going according to schedule, though the details were somewhat confused and occasionally contradictory. The Americans claimed that the Russians were conducting a scorched earth

58

policy as they left. The Moscow news agency Tass said that the mujahideen continued to harass Soviet convoys taking supplies through the Salang Tunnel to an increasingly beleaguered Kabul. Then we heard that the Afghan army was consolidating its positions round the capital, where no more than 1,000 Soviet troops remained in the garrison, with another 20,000 still waiting to be pulled out of Herat and surrounding district in the west of the country. The same BBC bulletin said that all those men were expected to leave within the next four days, and that the Russians would continue to airlift supplies into Kabul even after their soldiers had gone, so as to prevent the city's total collapse. Twenty-four hours later, *Pravda* reckoned that the last Soviet soldier was out of Kabul, the final column having come down the Salang Highway, where only two men were lost, both killed by an avalanche. From Herat, two columns were heading for the border and home. Meanwhile, in Islamabad, Benazir Bhutto and Eduard Shevardnadze were discussing the best ways of bringing peace to Afghanistan after almost a decade of war; and there was other momentous news. Mr Gorbachev was to visit China in spring, while Andrei Sakharov was going to Italy and Austria even earlier, to collect honorary degrees. In Hungary they were planning to exhume Imre Nagy from his anonymous grave and give him a decent funeral at last.

The world was beginning to shift on its axis as it had not done for a generation and more, while my own lifetime was looking like the most eventful period of history since the great European upheavals of the late eighteenth century. As I watched those troop transports gliding slowly down out of the sunset, I was acutely aware that this was yet another point at which, in a sense, that army's path and mine had converged. This was a most improbable conjunction, yet it seemed to have become a small destiny in my life. That I still thought of it as the Red Army – which had not been its proper title since 1947 – marked me as a child of the age into which I was born, even more decisively than absent-minded references to things happening before or after 'the war'; as though 1939–45 was the only period of conflict the world had known in the past fifty years.

I was first conscious of that Red Army as the winter of 1939 began, and with it the Russo–Finnish War. An enterprising teacher at my school had acquired a map of Europe on which we were planning to follow the course of our own hostilities with the Germans – 'the war' – by pinning up paper replicas of the Union Jack, the French Tricolour and the Nazi swastika to mark the various front lines: and she improvised some others, so that we could take note of Finland's Mannerheim Line and the Red Army's advance across Lake Ladoga, in the sideshow at the top of the map. This didn't last long before the Finns were forced to sue for peace after fighting most bravely against over-powering odds. Another cliché of the propaganda was that they had been overwhelmed by Bolshevik hordes. I remembered this well some fifteen months later, when the Germans attacked the soldiers of that same Red Army, who were instantly transformed in the public prints and on the BBC into our gallant Soviet allies. Shortly afterwards my school was addressed by a man whose expressed intention even then was to become a parliamentary candidate for the local constituency in the first post-war election, whenever that might be. In question time after his pep talk about fighting the good fight and why we must win, I precociously asked him how the unspeakable hordes of one minute could turn into the gallant allies of the next, and he said it was all a matter of perspective, but said nothing at all about telling the truth, which was what had been exercising my anxiously scrupulous young mind.

Nevertheless, I became the Red Army's most faithful ten-year-old liegeman in the North of England, I imagine, as I listened to the frightening news coming out of the eastern front in that bitter winter of 1941. There are some names on the map of Russia and the Ukraine that, even now, I cannot hear without a sense of anguish and impending doom, for when they were first uttered to me they meant yet another petition I must make in an attempt to turn the course of the war and halt that long litany of disasters: at Minsk and Ostrov, at Smolensk and Gomel, at Vitebsk and the Pripet Marshes, at Kharkov and the Donets, at Dnepropetrovsk and Novgorod, at Velikye Luki and Kiev, at Perekop and Bryansk, at Orel and Vyazma, at Taganrog and Kursk, right up to the gates of Moscow itself.

"Please, God," I used to pray every time another town fell to Guderian's panzers, "please, God, let this be a terrible winter in Russia, so that the Red Army can beat the Germans."

For I well understood what warfare on the eastern front amounted to, even as a juvenile. There were newsreels at the cinema that showed the mud and the snow and the bodies lying frozen stiff, the smoking ruins of homes that had been put to the torch, the corpses hanging broken-necked from gallows, where they had been strung up in reprisal for standing their ground in their own village streets. I knew that I was watching a nation on its way to extermination, whereas all we had to put up with was rationing and bombs. I understood the nightmare of Leningrad, even though I did not then know how its citizens had been reduced to eating earth mixed with sugar, then their pet animals, then their own dead. I agonised over the destruction of Stalingrad, felt profound relief when the enemy was at last thrown out of its ruins, and still think it was a shabby act to rename the city later so as to increase Stalin's disgrace, for it had a noble ring that was all its own. The Red Army meant nobility and courage and tenacity, too, in all that it did in those years. So much did I feel nothing but admiration and gratitude for its contribution to the war, that when my stepfather returned from his own fairly uneventful military service, he found me absorbed in some quite persuasive literature put out by the Anglo–Soviet Friendship Society. He forbade me to have it in the house. He knew which side his bread would be buttered on after 1945, and he didn't want to be seen fostering a young communist.

There was no real danger of that, though I never allowed myself to forget the price the Soviet Union had paid in the

61

alliance against Hitler, hideously higher than the cost to anyone else. And on this journey through Central Asia I had already discovered that the bonding of that time had not been forgotten here. At the Kazakh collective that had once been the women's prison camp, Evgeni and I had been given a feast, in which a score or more of us sat at a long table that sagged under the weight of salads and cheeses and noodle soup and meat and potatoes and pilau and varieties of bread and pancakes and sour cream and apples and toffees-to-finish-off-with. As I prepared to weigh into this banquet I was saddened only by the absence of wine or spirits, for although each place had a glass laid, the bottles on the table contained nothing stronger than mineral water. Then ladies appeared with huge teapots and I was asked whether I would like ak-chai or kara-chai – whether I preferred my tea white or black. Puzzled when I saw a colourless liquid poured into my glass, and by the giggling that had begun all round, I was gratified to discover that the choice was between brandy and vodka; and that this strange manoeuvre was an attempt to satisfy the collective thirst while at the same time observing the letter of Mr Gorbachev's injunction, that sought to discourage bottles of strong liquor on occasions such as this.

Before the meal was half-way through the room was ringing with animation, and when the time came for speeches, rambling dissertations had become inevitable. Toast followed toast, and one was made specifically to me by the director. Three generations ago his family had moved to Kazakhstan from the Ukraine, which probably meant that they were retracing some ancestral steps; for he had the wide cheekbones of many Slavs, indicating that some Tartar blood was introduced during those two hundred years of the Mongol conquest. The director started by reviewing the day's events, but what he really wanted to say to me was that he had been a boy of sixteen when the Great Patriotic War began, joined the Red Army as a volunteer, and fought with it all the way to Dresden.

He had always remembered that time; and one other

thing. "We knew how Englishmen were fighting the Fascists, how they were helping us, how they resisted them and did not let them land, despite heavy bombings." Applause all round the table at that. "We must be friends in order not to repeat what we went through then. We must meet and come to see each other frequently. Give our regards to Margaret T'atcher . . . "

At which the room erupted with acclaim.

Parental anxiety about incipient communism had been unnecessary in 1945, and I put the Red Army out of my mind soon afterwards, when it was subsumed into the dull aggressions of the Cold War. Not until 1968 did Russian troops engage my attention closely again. Early that year I found myself in Prague when the hard-line communism of Antonin Novotny was rejected by the Czechs, who anointed Alexander Dubček in his place and began to construct an ideology they called democratic socialism, which soon found itself in no-man's-land. For weeks I followed and participated in the Prague Spring, gave it my best wishes, identified with it, and wondered whether it would be allowed to last without interference from Moscow and elsewhere in the eastern bloc. I also fell in love with the city itself, which seemed to me a very model of what European civilisation at its best was capable of. I spent hours on the heights of Hradçany, gazing at the layers of pink pantiled roofs tumbling down to the Vltava, and just as many in the middle of the Charles Bridge, looking up at that heavenly skyline. I pottered among the tipsy graves in the old Jewish Cemetery and pursued Kafka among the galleried backyards of Stare Mesto. The Tyl Theatre, even without a production of *Don Giovanni* that season, was a delight and everywhere I walked I felt nothing but a great gladness that the war had spared all this. Suffused in the spirit of that year, which Comenius as well as Masaryk would have recognised, Prague was no less than a form of perfection to me.

I was sitting with friends in a café on Na Prikope when someone came in with a worried frown to say that the Russians were up to some trick or other. The Warsaw Pact manoeuvres had been held in Czechoslovakia that year, they had ended, and the Hungarians, the Poles, the East Germans and the rest had packed up and gone home; but not the Red Army, which was taking an inordinate time to strike camp and move out. *Rude Pravo* later that week came out with a cartoon, captioned 'Soviet troops leave Czechoslovakia.' It showed a column of tanks driving off to the east, disappearing into the hills at the frontier between the two countries; but if you looked more closely, you could see that the head of the column was reappearing from behind a hill at the end, on its way back. Eventually the army did leave, and another form of bullying was tried. I was with thousands in the Old Town Square, beneath the statue of Jan Hus, the night the Czech Praesidium returned from being browbeaten by the Soviet Politburo in the railway-man's institute on the frontier at Cierna nad Tisou. Josef Smrkovsky, who was the strong man behind Dubček, stood on a balcony opposite the statue and made a passionate speech in which he implored everyone not to provoke the Russians any more, especially in the derisive cartoons and articles which the Czech press, intoxicated by its new freedom to say what it liked, was publishing in every edition.

The day before the Praesidium left Prague for the frontier talks, a very remarkable thing had happened in the capital. The newspaper of the Writers' Union, *Literarny Listy*, had published a special number with a manifesto by the playwright Pavel Kohout, addressed to Dubček and his colleagues. Its burthen was that there comes a time in the affairs of small nations when they must stand up to overweening big ones defiantly, at whatever cost. This time had now come for Czechoslovakia, whose people begged their leaders to stand firm on their behalf. "Do not fail us. We will never fail you." Then followed the names and other identifications of hundreds who subscribed to these sentiments, in column after column of small type which filled the four pages of newsprint. All over Prague that afternoon small tables were set up, with blank sheets of paper on which others could sign their names, which would all be presented to the politicians before they flew off; and wherever there was a table, there was a long queue, as the autographed sheets of foolscap began to mount into pile after pile. My copy of that day's *LL*, its paper now discoloured after twenty years, has hung framed on the wall above my desk ever since.

After the browbeating by the Russians alone, there was the false bonhomie of every stool-pigeon in the Warsaw Pact at talks in the Slovakian capital, Bratislava; after which we all thought the Prague Spring would extend into what was left of summer and beyond, believing this so thankfully and confidently that I left for home at last. I was not there when the Soviet armour rolled across the Vltava's bridges on that base night of August 21st. I was not to see Prague again for another decade. Once more I watched the Red Army in action through the medium of film, but this time I did not admire. Nor were contempt and anger my only responses, even though the gallant allies had been translated into invading hordes again. Unspeakable the invasion was, but there was something in the manner of those troops that aroused something of pity for them, which stood apart from my much greater grief for the Czechs. There was a tank in Wenceslas Square one day, standing still with its hatches open, its crew looking out on the crowd surrounding it. In letters home to Moscow and Kharkov and Vitebsk the soldiers probably referred to those students and those housewives and those factory hands as a mob, for they were shouting angrily and shaking their fists; while two brave young people, crouched low where they were hidden from the crew's sight, were actually attaching the tank's towing hawser to its own tracks, so that when it rolled away it would be liable to strip them off and cripple itself. The crew were obviously waiting for fresh orders which, had they been to open fire, would have resulted in a massacre. Meanwhile they just sat and looked stunned, miserable, oppressed; above all, bewildered. I saw that look time and again on the faces of the Red Army that year in Prague.

Those troops had been told that they were going to rescue their socialist comrades from counter-revolutionary oppression organised by the wicked capitalists. And when they reached Prague they discovered it was a lie. Every socialist comrade in sight was telling them to clear off, back where they came from. They were not wanted there.

One more episode had prepared me to encounter in the flesh at last the old Red Army on active service. When I was exploring the North-west Frontier during my journey through Pakistan, just three years had elapsed since the Soviet Union had sent its troops into Afghanistan to establish and maintain the regime of Babrak Karmal against the various factions opposing it. Although it was by no means in control of a country which, because of its topography and its traditions, had never been controllable according to European notions of government, the regime and the Soviet troops still held the upper hand against the mujahideen, who were fighting the sort of guerrilla war that Afghans have always been most successful at. The initiative was still with the regime in 1983 partly because the mujahideen had not yet been adequately armed with modern weapons by the United States, through the agency of Pakistan, as they would be later; and partly because they were too often at each other's throats, when they needed uncompromising unity if they were to prosecute their holy war successfully. It sometimes seemed that the only thing they had in common was a detestation of the foreign invader, but that this alone was not powerful enough when set against their deadly jealousies, both tribal and personal, and their different aims for Afghanistan when at last the regime was toppled and the invader was turned back. These ranged from the most oppressive form of theocracy, modelled on the Ayatollah Khomeini's version in Iran, to a sort of Islamic democracy which did not exclude the possibility that ex-King Zahir might be invited home from exile in Italy to pose as a constitutional figurehead. In this situation, the mujahideen's successes were more or less confined to brilliant hit-and-run raids on Soviet convoys and isolated garrisons; but they suffered terribly when the highly-equipped army came after them in vengeance.

In Peshawar one day I met a young French doctor who had returned after months of running a field hospital for the muj, a resourceful and compassionate man who had experienced a counter-attack by the Soviet troops. He told how you would hear a distant hum, which caused you to look down the valley between the mountain walls. There you would see this great armada of helicopters flying steadily towards you, and your stomach would turn over at the sight. The choppers flew in an immense box formation, with transports containing many infantry in the middle, surrounded by gunships with a wicked amount of armament. They were looking for you and the people you were with, and in every single helicopter there were men with field glasses searching the ground for the slightest movement, for the tiniest gleam of light reflected from glass or metal in the burning sun. If they spotted anything, gunships sprayed the ground with fire from above for minutes on end. Then, and only then, the transports would lower themselves ominously and the platoons of infantry would leap out to search the landscape for anything left alive. They were there to kill you and your friends. They did not take prisoners. Nor did the mujahideen, except for a propaganda exercise now and then. These helicopter sorties were quite the most terrifying thing, said Gilles. Much worse than the rocket attacks, or the raids by aircraft which sprinkled the ground with anti-personnel devices that, if touched, might blow a man to bits or merely tear off an arm or a leg. The rockets and the air raids were over and done with quickly. The helicopter sorties happened slowly and deliberately, so that you were menaced for an hour or even more, while you lay hidden and paralysed with fear.

I saw some results of taking on the armed might of the Soviet Union in the mountains of Afghanistan. In a Peshawar hospital one ward after another was full of men who had lost limbs in the fighting. Some lay with eyes closed, motionless beneath sheets which outlined the shape of the body but sagged where part of it was missing. Others sat in chairs beside their beds, their amputated legs terminating in a dressing or, if the wound had healed, in a smooth pink dome. One bearded Pathan who had lost both legs had one of his stumps fitted into the cup of a Jaipur Foot, the crude artificial limb of leather, metal and wood that alone was serviceable in the hills, because it could be mended by a village blacksmith if any part of it broke. As I passed him, he was struggling to strap his other stump into a second appliance, grunting with the effort and not responding to my salute. Like all the wounded, he had been brought to the hospital by relatives, in a desperate journey across the mountains. Some wounded were conveyed by horses, mules or camels for a week or more before they reached sanctuary in Pakistan. My Pathan had somehow survived a ten-day forced march with shattered legs, carried piggy-back by each of his brothers in turn. It was quite possible that, when he had mastered his artificial limbs and become mobile again, he would go back across the mountains to fight the Russians; for this was jihad, the most fanatical kind of war. Allah, said a doctor at the hospital, was very strong for them.

Others would never walk again, let alone fight. A second hospital was full of paraplegics, whose spines had been irreparably damaged by Kalashnikov bullets or, more often, by bomb splinters. Their legs swung uselessly, like those of marionettes, as they moved about on crutches or on special walking frames, while their urine sloshed and foamed in waste-bags that each man carried attached to his side. It was not only the use of their legs that had been destroyed. These Afghan guerrillas – this belligerent mixture of Pathans, Tadzhiks, Uzbeks, Hazaras and others – set even greater store on their masculinity than most males in the Muslim world; but they were, in every sense, finished as virile men. So were some boys I saw in that hospital, who had not yet reached puberty before they were maimed in this way. Many of them had been injured when taking part in the ambush of a Soviet tank or armoured troop carrier. It was the habit of the mujahideen to have small boys run up to these with their hands full of dung, which they then smeared over the vehicle's solitary window, so that the driver could not see where he was going. When a soldier emerged from the hatch to clean away the mess, he was gunned down by the hidden kinsmen of the small boy. But sometimes the soldiers were quicker on the draw and shot the child from inside the tank before he could perform his task. It was, one way and another, what the military connoisseurs call a dirty war.

And now, six years later, after the tide of that war had turned, after the mujahideen had inflicted great losses on the Soviet troops – who admitted to more than 13,000 killed, another 35,000 injured – the Kremlin had swallowed its pride and decided to quit, in a downfall as humiliating as Napoleon's retreat from Moscow, as mortifying as the American withdrawal from Vietnam. Flying into Dushanbe that evening were conscripts who themselves might have maimed small boys such as the ones I had seen in Pakistan, and reduced fierce tribesmen to truncated wrecks. One or two of them were possibly the sons of young soldiers who had looked bewildered after invading Prague. Every one was almost certainly the grandson of some veteran who had served civilisation well in their Great Patriotic War. As I prepared to go in search of supper that evening, I was nervous at the prospect of encountering these soldiers, whose pedigree was so muddled, attractive and repellent to me in turn. I was not at all sure how I was going to react to any I might come across, and I was becoming uneasy at the prospect of a confrontation that my curiosity welcomed but that otherwise I could have done without. For it would require me to adopt a position, to express a judgment, and I was not certain, even now, what my position was.

The restaurant Evgeni and I found was the biggest and most popular in town, and it was very full by the time we arrived. We were placed at one of only two empty tables and the other seemed to have been abruptly abandoned, for there were plates with half-eaten food on them, a bottle of wine still had plenty in it, and two or three glasses were almost full. The dance floor in the middle of the room was not in use, though it soon would be, for the band had just come onto the stage above it and was tuning up. The twang of the electric guitars and the rumble and thump of chords on the electronic organ rose above the hubbub of conversation everywhere. I was intrigued by a party sitting between us and the stage; three very beautiful Tadzhik girls accompanied by a solitary male, all of them in Western clothes. The young man may have been Tadzhik too, though he was frail-looking compared with the girls, and his features were aquiline. He looked as though he'd had plenty to drink and his mouth had slackened into a self-satisfied leer. The moment the band launched into its first number he grabbed two of the girls and led them onto the floor, where he began to dance rather well, with a cigarette between his teeth, and his arms waving in the air like fronds of seaweed in a tide. When he had finished he led the girls to their place again, then he kept on walking to the far end of the room and disappeared for a moment or two. Sauntering back he made a detour to the empty table where, with the quickness of a striking snake, he snatched up the bottle of wine as he went past. His leer had become triumphant when he sat down with this loot, but the three girls appeared perfectly happy in his company, though I noticed that they carefully did not keep up with his intake of drink.

I first spotted the soldiers when this pimp, or whatever he was, left the room after that first dance. There were three of them, all in civilian clothes and all with hair that had been cropped into the caste style of the squaddie every-where. They sat very quietly and were extremely polite to the waitress serving them, not even mildly flirtatious, though she was attractive and paid them more attention than most of her customers. They were fresh-faced boys, one of them with a blond moustache, and while they did not in the least make a show of toughness they looked as though they had learned to take care of themselves. They spoke little to each other, seemed content to watch every-thing around them, and whatever they looked at was sub-jected to a very steady gaze. Two of them, in particular, kept throwing glances at the Tadzhik girls, and when the pimp took only one of his trio onto the floor, the soldiers rose together without a word and walked across to the remaining pair. Each boy stood over his chosen partner and bent down so closely that his mouth was almost touching her ear, to ask for the dance. The girls, who did not appear to have seen them until this moment, looked up and smiled, rose at once and took the offered hands. If they spoke at all while they moved together through two numbers I did not notice it. When the band rested the soldiers took the girls back to their seats, thanked them formally, and resumed their own. The strange Tadzhik foursome continued its desultory table talk until the leering male, who was either hyperactive or bent on demonstrating his way with women, selected another partner from the three and led her to dance once more.

Another figure now intervened. Sitting alone at a distant table was a man much older than any of these, possibly forty or so. He wore a neat grey suit, had his hair oiled into a quiff above a lean and weatherbeaten face, with slightly hooded eyes that had been watching the girls for some time, hungrily. When two of them were again alone, he moved directly to the prettier one and not only asked her to dance, but with an old-fashioned gesture withdrew her chair so that she could rise more easily. No other man that evening had done such a thing. On returning he again assisted her in the same way, then went back to his own seat. Still his gaze never left her, until a flower-seller entered the restaurant and began to move among the tables, doing business at almost every one. The man motioned her over, bought a dozen carnations, and asked her to take them to the girl he had danced with, whose table had now been rejoined by its lord and master. Hitherto he had been extremely offhand with the girls, whose duty was obviously to admire and flatter him. The moment the flowers arrived, his manner changed. He was suddenly all attention, his leer showing a little ardour rather than unalloyed conceit. He leaned towards the girl and said something, and she responded by stroking his shoulder reassuringly. Not once

71

did he look at the source of the flowers; nor did the girl acknowledge them. I would have given much to see her face at this point, but she had her back to me and to her admirer, whose eyes never left her. The soldiers, too, had been watching all this time without saying a word. They stared coolly, enigmatically, without a flicker of reaction. It was impossible to tell what was going through their minds.

By this time two other soldiers had arrived, swaying as if drunk, but one more in control than the other, whose eyes were no longer focusing properly. His arm was firmly in the grip of his mate, and the pair of them stood beside the stage uncertainly until two more squaddies arrived and they all waited for someone to direct them to the empty table, which had still not been cleared. Unlike the three who had been settled in for some time, these four were clad in a sort of uniform: identical stone-washed denim jackets with studs around the shoulders and fur-lined. It looked as if it might have been the standard off-duty rig in Kabul during the winter; and when one peeled off his jacket, it was to reveal a tee-shirt of thin blue hoops, which meant that he belonged to the airborne assault force, almost certainly the troops who flew the helicopter sorties that had so terrified my French doctor Gilles. He was the one who had been holding up his comrade and I studied him closely, for he had a good, strong face, with a fetching grin, certainly European but not strikingly Slav. Whatever he had been through lately, a drink or two had put him completely at his ease tonight. One could see how the others might be in the habit of depending on him: it would be he, I guessed, who would decide when they'd all had enough. The other three looked totally drained, still tense, too exhausted to do anything but sip beer and look around them, and feel safe.

I could imagine what the last day or two must have been like for them. They would have had no sleep since Friday night, maybe not even then. They would have been stood-to all yesterday and all last night, waiting for the order to move out to the airport in Kabul. Aboard the troop transport, there would have been the dangerous time – maybe half an hour

– after take-off, until they cleared the border between Afghanistan and the Soviet Union, when they could have been hit by a parting shot from a missile in the mujahideen's now sophisticated weaponry. They needed to signify their safety by some sort of night on the town, the moment they were stood down in Dushanbe. But what they needed most of all was rest, and time to unwind. They communicated with no one, scarcely even with each other. They sat wearily over their beers, quietly asked the waitress for some food; were so unobtrusive that I doubt whether many people in that restaurant even noticed them.

"They're very well behaved," I said to Evgeni.

"But of course. They're very well disciplined," he answered; with just enough smugness for me not to add what was going through my head. Which was that I could not imagine British or American troops behaving like this, if they had just flown from Kabul and what had gone before. Our boys, most of them at any rate, would have told themselves that they deserved a party after what they had been through and they would have had one, however weary they were. It would have been very noisy and rather drunken, and some of them would have smashed something or got into a fight or insulted some bystander or otherwise made a nuisance of themselves.

Not one soldier in that restaurant did any of those things during the three hours that I sat toying with my meal, spinning it out so that I could keep my eyes on them. At their two tables they slowly masticated their food and drank their beer, and watched the Tadzhik girls longingly, but did not dance again with any of them. Nor did the older man who had sent the flowers to the one he wanted. After a while he got up and left without a sign to her, conceding that his pursuit had been profitless. The pimp, after the arrival of the flowers, never left her side; and when he wanted to dance he took all three girls onto the floor, switching from one to another and making sure that the other two were always coupled together close by. I was not comfortable with the thought, but it seemed to me that every one of those soldiers, whatever part they had played in the dirty war they had just left behind, was much more wholesome than him.

I was awakened more than once during that night by the sound of planes coming in to land, and next day the town was full of troops fresh from the historic retreat. They were to be seen in their khaki battledress, walking the streets in twos and threes, or rummaging in the department stores for things they had been unable to buy in Kabul. Their choice here was sadly limited, too, as Evgeni found out when he went in search of brown shoe-laces but could obtain only white. Many necessities were in short supply, yet food appeared to be plentiful and of good quality, especially in the market, where stall after stall was loaded with tempting pyramids of fruit and vegetables. Burly men with beards presided over these, as well as the other commodities including a row of cradles like the one I had seen holding a baby inside the yurt. A huge patriarch, tall and strong but blind, stood foursquare on a corner with his arms garlanded with strings of beads, intended not for adornment but for meditation; for these were elfeeya, the rosaries of Islam. Every stallholder on that market was Muslim and Tadzhik, whether he was wearing the traditional skullcap with headcloth wound round it, or the ear-flapped fur hat. Some were dressed in long cloaks, not unlike the Arab djellaba, but coloured in stripes through every shade in the spectrum; akin, perhaps, to the biblical coat of many colours that Jacob wore.

I watched to see how they would respond to the soldiers strolling round their stalls, for their Soviet patriotism had been sorely tested by the war in Afghanistan. It is doubtful whether any Tadzhik, other than the party's placemen in authority, had been wholeheartedly in favour of the invasion of 1979. For history had left Tadzhiks untidily on both sides of the frontier, as it had Uzbeks, Kirghiz, Turkmen and one or two other tribes. The most glamorous of all the mujahideen commanders, Ahmad Shah Massoud, was a Tadzhik who had wrought havoc against the military up the Panjsher Valley of Afghanistan. Such a strain had been put upon divided loyalties that, after a few years of the war, Soviet conscripts from the Central Asian republics had no longer been sent into battle over there. That is why the young soldiers in the market were Slavs to a man, just as they had been the night before in the restaurant. The stallholders, not so very distant kinsmen of an enemy that had repulsed this mighty army and sent it home chastened as never before, scrutinised the battledresses with neither more nor less interest than they showed any other prospect of trade. In the town, as a whole, there was little emotion at the homecoming. Just once I saw a man cross the street to shake hands demonstratively with a couple of lads in fighting rig. They looked grateful but embarrassed; and he, too, was a Slav.

As it happened, the only veteran of the war that I talked to was not one of these Russians, but an Uzbek I met in different circumstances a little later; and Evgeni's native caution was the principal reason why I was inhibited from approaching soldiers who had only just returned from the front. My companion's view of the war was very close to that of every Russian I discussed it with. It had been a terrible blunder, a costly mistake in terms of casualties, of expenditure and of the Soviet Union's reputation in the world. Evgeni, in fact, was the only person who gave me the impression that a moral question was also at issue here: otherwise, I found myself wondering whether these hostilities would have been condemned so roundly if the mujahideen, rather than the Army, had been forced to concede defeat.

In the restaurant my impulse had been to engage some of the soldiers in conversation, an idea that had agitated my friend. He raised his hand in horror and it palpitated in his anxiety to repudiate my suggestion.

"No, no, no," he stuttered, "I really must advise you against such an impetuous course. There would be a grave danger of its being misconstrued and ... " he was now shaking his head rapidly too, "other difficulties might then present themselves."

His alarm was so manifest that I deferred to him, and felt a twinge of sympathy for the position he was in. He was a bookish person, not a bureaucrat; a senior editor in the principal state publishing house. For all that he had Moscow's authority to wield on my behalf, there were areas I could well imagine his wanting to keep well away from except in extremis, especially anything remotely connected with national security. Evgeni had, after all, been reared in the Soviet Union of Stalin and Beria, when innocent people could be accused and found guilty of subversion on the slightest pretext, or none at all.

A couple of weeks later, however, an opportunity presented itself. In the countryside, whenever I was invited into someone's home and conversation ranged over general matters affecting the life of the community, I invariably slipped in some mild questions about the war. They must be glad it was now over, living so close to the border? Yes, they were very relieved. I expected that some of the local boys had done their service in Afghanistan like everybody else? One or two, but all, thank God, had come safely home. Had they been much affected by their experiences? Some had returned much more nervous than they had been before. The questioning never became more detailed than this, nor did any young serviceman ever appear in person so that I might ask him point blank how things had been.

But on this occasion we were walking down a street when, on rounding a corner, we came to the local forge. A man with a jet-black mop of hair and moustache, still on the right side of thirty, I guessed, was beating a piece of red-hot metal on an anvil. An adolescent who looked like his brother was raising the smithy fire to white-heat with a pair of bellows. The older man smiled when I greeted them, flashing a grin whose upper half consisted entirely of gold teeth, which met a full complement, perfectly formed, of natural white ones underneath. I asked if he would mind if I stopped to watch him at work for a while, and he gestured me to enter. He lay down his blacksmith's maul and pincers, found a piece of newspaper, and wiped clean a couple of boxes, motioning us to sit there.

Our talk at first was of his craft, and how it compared with practices in other lands I knew. Mostly he was making knives and agricultural tools, like the drawhoe blade he was beating into shape at that moment; there was little call for horseshoes round there. I told him of the blacksmith's shop in my own village at home, how it had adapted to plumbing when the horse was displaced by the tractor, but how one of the old men could remember the time when not only horses but cattle would be shod, so that they could be driven along the hard roads between Scotland and markets in the English Midlands. What's more, I said, although there was only one smithy in the village today, well within memory there had been no fewer than four. That had been just after the war, when there was but one tractor in the dale, most implements still being powered by the horse.

"Which war would that be?" asked the smith, bent again to his task.

"The one you call the Great Patriotic War," I replied. "Not the one you fought in."

He looked up quickly and stared at me very hard for an instant; then slowly smiled. "Massoud was supposed to ride about on a beautiful black horse," he said, "but I never got close enough to see."

Gingerly I began to question him about his war, and there was no hesitation once he had decided to talk. He answered carefully, remembering, choosing his words, his expression changing from time to time.

He had been conscripted into the army in 1981, when he was just twenty, and the invaders still held the upper hand after a couple of years' fighting. He hadn't been a soldier long before he was involved in a fight with a sergeant, in the course of which he kicked the man in the head and knocked him cold. The smith grinned happily at the memory. He was put on a charge, and the officers pointed out that it was quite impossible to have him and the sergeant in the same unit any more; and he could see the sense in that. Would he, they asked him, like to serve somewhere nearer home for the rest of his time? He grinned again, but faintly now. " 'Sure,' I said, 'that'll do me fine. Thank you very much.' " Twenty-four hours later he was in Kabul, and he stayed in Afghanistan without a break until his demobilisation in 1983. But for the first six months his family had no idea where he was, beyond the fact that he was in 'a border area,' because his letters home were stopped.

Within a day of arriving he was in action, and by the time his service was over the smith had been in no fewer than 161 engagements with the mujahideen; about twice every week. He had also been promoted to sergeant and he had won a medal for bringing his men to safety after the platoon had found themselves surrounded up in the hills. He spoke of this with a touch of bravura, and much glinting of gold teeth.

"Did you kill men?" I asked.

"Sure I killed men. That's what I was there for."

"How many?"

"Twelve or fourteen that I know of."

"How?"

"Kalashnikov."

I felt like a voyeur, as I had when I questioned the wounded muj in the hospital. The smith was without bravura when he counted those dead. He sounded a little sad, but with a shrug in his voice. He did not call his enemies mujahideen. He referred to them as basmatchi, which usually means bandit and was first applied by the Bolsheviks to the Muslim nationalists – some quite possibly the smith's own predecessors – who rose against them in Central Asia in 1920. Apart from the basmatchi he had killed, there would probably be others he had damaged for life; perhaps even small boys like those I had seen in Peshawar. He was fighting in Afghanistan when I was just a few miles away at the southern end of the Khyber Pass, and, even closer, up in Chitral.

But there was another side to that coin, and the smith's voice dropped almost to a mutter when he spoke of it. One man in his unit had been acting as sentry during a night watch, and he disappeared. They found his body two weeks later, with its eyes missing, its heart cut out, a hand amputated.

I was half prepared to be told something like that. Similar stories were current in the British Army before 1947, about atrocities committed by the Pathans on the North-West Frontier. Sir Olaf Caroe, scholar as well as last imperial Governor of the North-West Frontier Province, had always gone out of his way to deny that Pathans ever employed torture "for its own sake," though he conceded that there was a long tradition among peoples of Turkic descent of blinding those to whom they were bitterly hostile. And I myself had been in Khartoum when a thief's hand was judicially amputated under Muslim Shariat law.

"Did you actually see this body yourself? Or did you just hear about it?"

"I saw it. With my own eyes."

"How had he been killed?"

The smith made a thrusting gesture, as if with a knife towards the heart.

The mutilations, he said, were reserved for the Russian, Ukrainian and Byelorussian boys. All that the Muslim soldiers in the Soviet Army had to worry about was collecting a bullet and being blown up. It was worse for troops of the Afghan Army, regarded by the mujahideen as the worst form of collaborator. One Afghan who had been captured by the muj was given a Kalashnikov and told to bring back two Russians, dead or alive, otherwise his family would suffer. He went to the smith's unit to ask for protection and for a month the Soviet troops guarded his wife and four children carefully. Then they were moved out to another sector. Within a week the family was slaughtered.

By the time the smith was due to be released from all this, half the regiment he had started out with in Kabul had been killed, many of them as a result of rocket attacks or being in the wrong place when a mine exploded. Sometimes there would be nothing at all left of a man, though there would be sizeable pieces of other bodies lying around. They would therefore distribute the pieces among coffins that had to tally with the number of men lost, so that all the relatives back home could believe they had received the remains of the son, the brother, the husband, the father, including the ones who had in fact been atomised. Grief had to be assisted along its proper course, even deceptively.

Those coffins dogged the blacksmith right to the end of his time in Afghanistan. The now decorated sergeant was due to fly home from Kabul on a Thursday, but the weather that day was foul and the flight was cancelled. So they put him aboard the solitary flight scheduled for Friday, known throughout the army as the Black Tulip because it took the weekly consignment of bodies out. The smith was the only living passenger on that plane. And when it touched down, he said, he did what he had promised himself he would do if he ever saw home again. He knelt down and kissed the Soviet earth.

It had been a very dirty war, and everyone who had shed blood in it would be tainted for the rest of his days. Yet I could not feel anger towards this sturdy man with the grotesquely golden smile, who had much confessed blood on his hands that were now merely grimed with decent toil. In spite of the fact that he had been deeply involved in the war, or maybe because of this and because he had come safely out of it, I felt again what I had experienced in Dushanbe, the night I saw the young soldiers who had been in the great retreat. My instinct had been to buy them a drink and wish them well.

4

A Desolation That Was Merv

The brown plain stretched to the horizon on all sides, under a pale blue sky and a warming sun. To the south there would eventually be mountains again, separating Turkmenia from both Iran and Afghanistan, but they were not in sight from here. To the north, the gravel of the plain soon ran into the sands of the Kara Kum desert, where dunes were sometimes 300 feet high and the camel came into its own. A camel was padding along the road on which we had paused, beast of burden for a Turkman with a large and untidy sheepskin busby on his head. It was an Arabian dromedary, as were all the camels bred in this part of the world. There were said to be a few Bactrians in Kazakhstan, but that shaggy, two-humped creature really belonged to Central Asia east of the Tien Shan. The man led the camel and its load of wood down the road, their feet shuffling up puffs of dust at every step. Their progress emphasised the desolation of the surrounding plain. Its flatness was broken by small piles and long ridges of rubble, where nothing but stunted bushes grew. Also by the occasional stump of masonry, the remains of a building, separated by great distance from the next and then the next after that. So isolated was each that collectively they caught the eye like a pattern of termite nests. And this was all that was left of ancient Merv.

Just out of sight was its successor, the dreary town whose name was changed from Merv to Mary in Stalin's time, another big garrison of the Russian military machine both before and since. The original Merv was much more considerable than that: this much we know, even allowing for the notorious difficulty in establishing historical fact in Central Asia. One unverifiable legend maintains that Merv was founded by Zoroaster, or Zarathustra, the Persian divine whose dates are usually given as 628–551 BC, and whose prophetic beliefs, once the religion of an empire, now survive chiefly among the Parsees of India. Just as speculative is the notion that Merv was where Scheherazade saved her life, when others had perished the morning after the night before, by telling Shahriyar the tantalising stories that in time became celebrated as *The Thousand and One Nights* (or *Arabian Nights*). What we do know is that this was an important staging post on the Silk Route, deriving from its position as an oasis on the edge of the desert. It was also an archbishopric of the Nestorian Church, whose fundamental assertion that there were two separate persons in the incarnate Christ, one divine and the other human, was denounced as heresy at the Council of Ephesus in AD 431; in spite of which the Church flourished from its base at Ctesiphon on the Tigris, and expanded across Asia for several hundred years. Merv was simultaneously headquarters of the most westerly province of the Sassanian rulers of Persia, whose dynasty collapsed at the seventh-century Islamic invasion of Central Asia. Yet Merv expanded and its reputation was much enlarged under Islam, especially when it became the capital of the Seljuk Turks, whose empire extended through Anatolia, Persia, Mesopotamia, Syria and Palestine. Even before the Seljuks, it was regarded as the second most important city in the known world, preceded only by Baghdad. It contained palaces, an observatory, many important libraries; and its artisans were so skilfully sophisticated that they could counterfeit the finest Chinese porcelain and despatch the pieces in the caravans bound for Europe, where connoisseurs mistook the forgeries for originals. It manufactured textiles in both cotton and silk, for export as well as local use. Merv in those days was a walled city, some fifteen miles in extent, from one side to the other. Even by the standards of today, it was a metropolis.

I had already visited other antiquities in the region, which bore no resemblance to this desolation. Much further west, beyond the Turkmenian capital of Ashkhabad, the great natural barrier which separated the Soviet Union from all other countries to the south had diminished to a range of hills whose sides were steep but not high enough to attract snow even at this time of the year. This range marked the frontier with Iran and sheltering below its northern slopes were the remains of old Nisa. Here had been the capital of the Parthians, whose empire lasted from 247 BC to AD 224 and extended from the Euphrates to northern India. The Parthians were notable for their horsemanship, a semi-nomadic warrior race who were also – according to a severely Classical authority, writing, and disapproving, at the beginning of our own century – "addicted much to drinking and to every manner of lewdness, and their laws permitted them to raise children even by their own mothers and sisters". The remarkable thing about Nisa was that a great deal of it was now visible above ground, having been preserved by drifting sand until archaeologists began to dig it out some thirty years ago. Walls had been exhumed, buttresses, pillars and cavities had been revealed; and although all detail had perished in the course of time, enough of Nisa had survived almost two thousand years to give us a reasonable impression of the community the Parthians had known. It looked a bit like an extensive sand castle on a beach, after the first wave or two of an incoming tide has started the demolition and blurred all the sharp outline.

At the site of ancient Merv, no such preservation had taken place. I had never seen such devastation as this, with only the occasional ruin standing to draw attention to the levelling that had generally occurred. The most exciting of these was the mausoleum of the Seljuk ruler, Sultan Mu'izz ad Din Sanjar, who died in 1157. Evgeni and I inspected it in the company of a woman from the museum in Mary, who was in charge of the restoration work being carried out on the building. The tomb had been enclosed within a huge brick cube from which rose an arched gallery and, above that, the drum of a double dome whose outer skin had once consisted of turquoise tiles so vivid that the mausoleum was visible to travellers a full day's journey across the desert from Merv. The tiles had long since vanished, and so had much else, but the restorers had repaired the cube's outer wall and the gallery above, until these were approximately in their original condition. A panel had been uncovered in the course of their work and hidden behind it was the name of the architect, 'Muhammad orphan from Sarakhs.' The archaeologists who went ahead of the restorers had also discovered that the foundations of the building had been sunk in the form of an inverted pyramid about forty-five feet deep, which they thought was done in order to minimise the effect of earthquakes, always a hazard hereabouts. As the orphaned Muhammad left it eight hundred years ago, this would have been a most handsome building as well as a sophisticated one. The Seljuk bricklayers would have been at work at the same time as master masons were starting to raise the cathedrals at Ripon in England, and at Notre Dame in Paris; and these Gothic marvels had not only survived to our own day in spite of revolutions and wars, but still functioned in the manner of their origins. In Asia the small masterpiece had virtually been destroyed long ago, its skeleton completely abandoned until now.

84

Nothing else in this wasteland had weathered the centuries even to that extent; and if it had not been for the restorations there would have been nothing at all to connect it to the present day. Historians are maddeningly vague about the shifting of Merv from its ancient site to another position several miles away, where modern Mary now is. But I had little doubt that I was contemplating the result of conquest by Genghiz Khan and his Mongolian hordes; though it was, in fact, the khan's youngest son Tolui who led the attack on Merv in February 1221, for the father was wintering near Balkh, over the mountains in Afghanistan.

Tolui brought his troops to the outskirts of the city and for six days made his preparations to besiege the walls with mighty catapults, mangonels and other appliances that the Mongols had copied from the Chinese. The Governor of Merv and its citizens remained defiant while the besiegers made ready; but on the seventh day, when Tolui gave the order to storm the city, the Governor's courage left him. He offered to surrender Merv if its people were spared, and Tolui accepted this. The gates were opened and the citizenry were driven out to where the Mongolian army awaited them, its soldiers under orders to behead between 300 and 400 victims apiece. Some artisans were spared for transportation to Mongolia and a life of slavery. Otherwise, everyone who could not escape was put to death. Some sources count the death toll as low as 500,000, others as high as a million, but all agree that this was one of history's most dreadful massacres. Sultan Sanjar's tomb was plundered and the adjacent mosque set on fire, as were the other buildings in the city, while its irrigation system was wrecked, effectively beyond repair. Then Tolui and his troops withdrew, laden with booty.

That some inhabitants had survived the initial horror is confirmed by what happened next. After making quite sure that the horde had gone, people crept back into the ruins, where they probably stood incapable of anything but dazed incredulity at what they found. That's when Tolui's army returned and killed all who had escaped their first onslaught.

It was an old ruse of Genghiz Khan's, and it never failed. After it had succeeded yet again, there was only a shocking wreckage left of what had lately been the second city in the world. The geographer Yaqut ibn Abdullah, who had spent many months studying in Merv's libraries some three years before these events, and afterwards visited the scene of the carnage, wrote that its splendid palaces and other buildings "were effaced from the earth as lines of writing are effaced from paper, and these abodes became a dwelling for the owl and the raven." Just over a century later, the great Arab traveller Ibn Battuta passed this way and confirmed that Merv, like Balkh, lay in ruins.

It is quite impossible to ignore the terrible genius of Genghiz Khan in Central Asia, for his shadow falls across the landscape wherever the wanderer goes. This was his heartland, where he was shaped by topography, climate and nomad society, as well as by his individual demon, into the mightiest of all warlords. He was not the first to emerge from this wilderness of mountain, desert and steppe, and to pillage civilisation: the Black Huns issued from the same source much earlier and dominated half Europe for several decades before the death of Attila in AD 453. But no one before Genghiz Khan had been capable of conquest on such a scale as he and his family, first seizing and then maintaining an empire which at one and the same time extended westwards to the middle of Europe and in the east to the shores of the Pacific: and no other leader has initiated such a feat since. His dynasty possessed half the known world before it expired. In order to do so, it defeated and demoralised European armies, Arab armies, Turkic armies, Persian armies, Chinese armies, Korean armies, Indian armies, Burmese armies. It then pacified the ravaged territories by a combination of cruelty, exaction, wisdom, tolerance and skilful administration. Genghiz Khan was not simply a vicious conqueror. His legacy was the Pax Mongolica, which lasted for almost a hundred years and was everywhere a period of exceptional tranquillity.

Another measurement of his stature is that the history of

86

the Mongols before Genghiz Khan is mostly a matter for conjecture; afterwards it was indelibly written into the history of the world. What we do know of the earlier period is that his people originated in a relatively small area to the east of modern Ulan Bator, between the rivers Onen and Kerulen. They worshipped a deity named Tengri, whom they often approached by climbing the nearest mountain for closer contact, because their concept of Tengri translates approximately as Eternal Heaven. Otherwise the shaman, the witch-doctor, was their normal intermediary for the supernatural, with his rituals, his exorcisms, his magic-makings. They had a profound reverence for the rising sun and they would habitually genuflect to the south, where it was at its height, as well as erecting their felt tents so that the doorway faced the south, too. Their superstitions forbade them to touch fire with a knife, and oaths were taken by drinking blood, sometimes by chopping a horse in two. Water was so sacred that nothing at all could be washed, which resulted in the total lack of hygiene for which the Mongols became notorious wherever they went.

The following description is by a Persian who observed the rare sight of Mongol prisoners taken during one of Genghiz Khan's campaigns:

Their eyes were so narrow and piercing that they might have bored a hole in a brazen vessel, and their stench was more horrible than their colour. Their heads were set on their bodies as if they had no necks, and their cheeks resembled leather bottles full of wrinkles and knots. Their noses extended from cheekbone to cheekbone. Their nostrils resembled rotting graves, and from them the hair descended as far as the lips. Their moustaches were of extravagant length, but the beards above their chins were very scanty. Their chests, in colour half-black, half-white, were covered with lice which looked like sesame growing on a bad soil. Their bodies, indeed, were covered with these insects, and their skins were as rough-grained as shagreen leather, fit only to be converted into shoes.

The Mongols were never very numerous, one estimate putting the total population in 1227 – when Genghiz Khan died – at no more than half a million. A reason for the wholesale slaughter at Merv and other conquered cities may well have been a need by the Mongols to ensure that immense numbers of enemies were not left in their wake, plotting revenge. Another imperative of the small community would explain why they were not only polygamous but exogamous as well; their tribesmen not merely urged, but required, to seek wives outside their own clans in order to remove the risk of the strain becoming enfeebled. The abduction of women was consequently commonplace, as was the warfare that followed between the tribes involved. And in warfare, the Mongol women went into battle alongside their men, to support them before and after, to reinforce them if necessary during the engagement. A demarcation line was drawn in the handling of animals. Women milked all she-beasts with the exception of mares, who were left to the men. Mare's milk was the most highly prized commodity of all after horseflesh, which was the staple food. It was fermented into an alcoholic drink called kumiss, and it was curdled into kurt, a solid form of iron rations for use by the armies on campaign.*

This was the world into which the great warlord was born in 1162. His father, leader of the Borjigin clan of Mongols, had lately killed a Tartar chief named Temujin and, according to custom, this was the name given to the Mongol's first son, who was born soon afterwards. Nine years later, the Tartars revenged themselves by poisoning Temujin's father

---

* Both substances survive in Central Asia today and I had tried them in Kazakhstan. Kumiss was not disagreeable, though its sourness contained a faint hint of vomit. I was offered kurt as a mild practical joke by Usmanova the day we attended the beauty contest, being told that it was a sort of sweet to follow the main meal. It looked like a creamy fudge and I had begun to chew a piece before I realised to my horror that my problem was not so much whether I would be able to get it down as whether I would be able to stop everything else coming up. It tasted exactly like a cowshed smells after the milking is done.

and the boy became the effective head of the family, with a mother, a stepmother, three brothers, a sister and two stepbrothers to find for. His life for the next twenty years or so becomes indistinct, apart from a few episodes which illustrate this period like a series of snapshots. For reasons that can only be guessed at – presumably to do with the succession in leadership – the widows and their brood are abandoned by the rest of the clan, which moves off elsewhere, probably for better horse pasture. Temujin quarrels with one of his stepbrothers and kills him. The man who has succeeded his father as chief of the clan captures the lad but he escapes. Thieves take most of the family's horses, the most grievous form of robbery among nomads, but Temujin retrieves them. At the age of fifteen he acquires a wife, who had been promised him just before his father's death. She is abducted soon after he has claimed her but, like the horses, she too is retrieved. He makes various friendships outside his immediate clan, which are to be of great value to him when he comes into his own, producing his most reliable aides. Other alliances are formed, while some earlier compacts are broken. Yet there are great gaps in the story of Temujin until he is about thirty-three years old and is hoisted to the leadership of the Mongols, with the title Genghiz Khan. Khan is an appellation familiar enough to the twentieth-century reader. But we still don't know what Genghiz means.

His first act on being elevated was to form a bodyguard which from then on protected him continuously, as long as he lived. At first it consisted of seventy men during the day and eighty when darkness fell. These were archers, swordsmen, sentries, messengers, and minders who were near him when he ate and when he slept. In battle one thousand special troops took up their formation round the khan and insulated him from all harm until victory was won. As his conquests mounted, as his name became more feared and hated than that of anyone else on earth, the strength of the bodyguard crept upwards until it stood at 10,000 men in all. Genghiz Khan was not the man to put himself at too much risk when he went to war. He did not ride with the vanguard, leading their charge: surrounded by his most trusted cohorts, he directed operations from some distance behind the front.

After creating a bodyguard, he systematically disposed of all possible rivals to his title, and the process was a messy one. There is an awful story in which, after vanquishing one chieftain, Genghiz Khan had seventy prisoners boiled alive, with a suggestion of cannibalism when they were cooked (and why stop at cannibalism when the Mongols were perfectly capable of augmenting their iron rations by drinking blood straight from the jugular veins of their steeds, or even of consuming the afterbirth of foals?). Several times the khan did not feel easy in his victories until every combatant who had opposed his army, whether wounded or merely abject, had been done to death. Occasionally he offered clemency to some individual, apparently on a whim. Often enough non-combatants were disposed of as brutally as the fighters. It was, after all, a generally cruel age, without mitigating affectations of chivalry. One of the few rules the Mongols observed was the one that forbade the spilling of chiefly blood except in battle. If a high-born man must be executed, then it meant strangulation with a bowstring, smothering under a heap of felts, or some other ingenious way of extinguishing life without butchery. When the shaman Kokochu threatened his leader's position, three men were ordered to put him down by breaking his back.

Kokochu was that perennial figure in world history, the man whose religious credentials secure him much influence at court, where he finally overreaches himself. It was Kokochu who had pronounced the divine blessing on Genghiz Khan, so that the khan could proclaim his own authority over all who dwelt in felt tents, raising his white standard with its nine yak tails to command allegiance in the encampment or on the battlefield. When he led his armies out of their Mongolian heartland for conquest further afield, those who trembled in the face of his advance tended to regard all these fierce yurt-dwellers as Mongols. In fact, the Mongol fighting force by then had become a complex mixture of many tribes which had been conquered by or assimilated into Genghiz Khan's native stock. Many were of Turkic origin, descended from those invaders who had reached the heartland some six hundred years earlier. Tartars formed such a high proportion of the soldiery that in Russia and eastern Europe the words Tartar and Mongol became interchangeable in the vocabulary of their victims. At the height of the empire the true Mongol kinsmen of Genghiz Khan and his sons provided the officer class, the rank and file coming from an assortment of Central Asian nomads.

The army was organised on principles which Genghiz Khan had not invented but had carefully refined from practices known in Central Asia long before his era. Its basis was the horse, domesticated here before anywhere else on earth five thousand years ago, and certainly introduced to warfare no later than 900 BC. By then, nomads ranging the steppe had learned how to control their horses so well with their legs and feet, without benefit of stirrups, that they were able simultaneously to draw bowstrings and fire arrows even when swivelling at the hip to aim at pursuers. By the thirteenth century it was probably quite true that most Mongols were able to ride a horse before they could walk properly. Every adult male was so inseparable from his mount that he was perfectly capable of sleeping in the saddle if need be. Because of their inbred stamina and because each rider never moved anywhere without two or three spare horses trotting alongside him, the Mongols could cover great distances at speeds unheard of in any other cavalry, before or since. Genghiz Khan took one of his armies 130 miles in two days on a campaign in 1221, and his general Subadai led another through deep snow for 180 miles in three days. These were, moreover, deadly marksmen at the gallop, able to hit their target in any direction at between 200 and 300 yards. Each man carried two bows for this purpose, one short-range, one long-range, and a couple of quivers with broad and slender iron-tipped arrows.

Eventually the Mongols developed a sort of artillery, so that they could more effectively besiege walled cities like Merv. They also employed an amount of infantry in time; and they had an unpleasant habit of marching prisoners in front of these, to take the first impact of an enemy's counter-attack. But what made Genghiz Khan and his commanders so terrifyingly successful in one campaign after another was, above all, their unprecedented superiority in cavalry warfare; not only in the basic skills of riding and fighting from horseback and in the speed with which they moved across difficult country, but in the ingenuity and cunning they brought to tactics and strategy. These were never large armies: it has been calculated that at the height of Mongol aggression in the first half of the thirteenth century, there could never have been more than 120,000 men in the field. Mongol commanders very often made their strength apparently greater than it really was by intelligent deceptions. They would advance in an extended but very thin line and leave the imagination of the enemy to suppose that many more horsemen were spread across the horizon, too, backing up the visible vanguard. They would even rig up dummy riders and lash these onto the backs of their spare mounts, in order to give the same impression. They sent their highly mobile scouts not only well ahead of their advancing tumens, but on the flanks as well, so that the commanders were always precisely informed of the enemy's disposition long before battle was joined. Sometimes the scouts were used as decoys to draw the enemy into some natural trap in the landscape, where he could be more easily destroyed than on the open steppe. A whole army would pretend to retreat, so that at an opportune moment it could turn, encircle and then annihilate a pursuing and unsuspecting foe.

Distance was of no consequence in such stratagems. Subadai once feigned a retreat for nine full days before turning and wiping out his pursuers. Nor did the Mongols care how far they themselves must ride in order to kill every last man who had fought them, sometimes being seen up to three hundred miles from the original action, still relentlessly tracking down their prey. This was no more than an extension of their life when not at war. Just as they improved their horsemanship by riding hard and tussling with each other over a sheep's carcass for relaxation, so they trained themselves to pursue an enemy inexorably by hunting animals for food and sport. Every so often Genghiz Khan would himself lead his squadrons in a highly organised and lengthy battue, whose immediate purpose was to kill enough food to see the troops through the winter; but the battues were conducted as tactical exercises and were in effect large-scale military manoeuvres.

There was no natural obstacle that could deflect this cavalry. When they came to a river they would remove their clothes, put them into leather bags they carried for this purpose, tie each bag to a horse's tail, and then every rider would swim across holding onto his steed. Nor was any season of the year a barrier to them. This remains the only army that has ever successfully invaded Russia in the depths of its winter. It was an army not only much tougher than any other it might meet, but one which was unrivalled in its discipline. When a city was taken, not a man laid a finger on any potential loot until the order was given by the commander. The Mongol training in the skills of war was so effective, the penalties for disobedience or even for making a mistake so severe, that no one needed telling what to do on the battlefield. An enemy was often thrown into panic merely by the sight of the Mongols approaching in absolute silence apart from the sounds of the horses and their gear. A black flag was raised on the left flank, and a hundred horsemen over there began to wheel onto a different course. In a night attack a torch would be lit over yonder, and anyone straining his eyes to detect movement would understand that unseen riders were already regrouping in a premeditated pattern, ready for the coup de grâce.

A night attack would be unnerving enough, but perhaps the sight of the Mongols coming towards you in broad daylight, mutely certain of their invincibility, without a twitch of compassion between them, each horseman a horribly efficient killer . . . perhaps this would be much more terrifying to those who awaited the onslaught and tried not to think of the Mongol reputation. In front would ride the general deputed by Genghiz Khan to lead the assault, in an armour of laminated leather strips which hung from his shoulders like a cloak, and in his iron helmet with great leather flaps. Beside him on a Bactrian camel would be the naccara, the great war drums hanging on either side of the beast, the drummer sitting poised to beat them and announce the final devastating charge. Behind these two would come the heavy cavalry, each horse and its rider coated in the leather armour, each horseman carrying a hooked lance in addition to his bow, so that he could pull an adversary from his horse without getting too close; for the Mongols avoided hand to hand combat whenever possible. Behind these and on the flanks would come the light cavalry, the mounted bowmen wearing the customary Mongol garb of fur hat with ear flaps, long hide coat turned inside out, and felted boots. Some of these riders would be swinging swords or axes as the measured walking of the horses broke into a trot, while others would reach for their quivers when the cantering began. Then the drummer would end the trembling silence, the naccara would boom, and the horde of Mongols would suddenly be galloping the last few hundred yards towards an enemy who had very little longer to live.

The first foreigners to experience the terrible efficiency of Mongol arms were the Ch'in rulers to the east of the heartland. Genghiz Khan's position was subordinate to that of the emperor in Peking, it involved annual tribute, and in 1211 he made war on the Chinese in order to end this indignity. The campaign was to continue for some time after his death sixteen years later, for it was an intermittent conflict, with truces between crushing Mongol victories, because the Chinese were so much more numerous than the invaders that they were able to repopulate an area very soon after it was devastated, and even Mongols needed a breathing space now and then. The war was prolonged in spite of the fact that Peking fell only four years after hostilities began, destroyed and sacked so brutally that a Persian ambassador who visited the scene shortly afterwards reported that its palaces and temples had all been demolished, while near one of the city gates was a colossal pile of bones, the remains of 60,000 girls who had flung themselves from the battlements rather than face the prospect of becoming Mongolian breeding stock. The emperor withdrew to the hinterland and some other Chinese were spared, most notably the men who could operate the siege machines the Mongols had never seen before, but very quickly learned to appreciate. Always their extermination of defeated foes was tempered by the shrewd selection of a few who would be useful to them alive.

The Chinese campaign established the pattern that would be followed to the end of the thirteenth century, at almost every point of the compass. After nominating his son Ogodei as heir apparent in 1218, Genghiz Khan left subordinates to carry on the war in China while he led other Mongol armies to new conquests in the west, for no other reason than the satisfaction of an aggressive appetite. Pouring through the Dzungarian Gate, an opening in the mountains that first of all allowed access to the Kazakh steppe, they fell upon the lands of Transoxiana that had once belonged to the Seljuk Turks but were now ruled by the Khwarizm Sultan Muhammad II. Genghiz Khan himself reduced the old oasis and caravan staging post of Bukhara to a rubble, with the exception of a single tower whose elegance impressed him so much that he allowed it to remain standing. He besieged the even more ancient city of Samarkand and, on taking it, treated its survivors in the customary fashion. Merv was meanwhile being disposed of by his son Tolui, with the results that I had seen. The armies spread south across the mountains into Afghanistan, and northwards across the desert to the steppe of southern Russia.

There was then a lengthy pause for consolidation, and in it Genghiz Khan died. He had recrossed the Amu Dar'ya – the River Oxus of Alexander the Great's time – had returned

95

to Mongolia and from thence had resumed the leadership of his eastern army in order to overcome a local impediment in the Chinese campaign. Early in 1227 the old warrior was thrown from his horse during a battue, and it is thought that internal injuries suffered in the fall probably caused his death six months later at the age of sixty-six. The body was carried from China home to the heartland, and it is said that the Mongols killed every human being they passed on the way. The burial took place somewhere on the sacred mountain of Burqan Qaldun, which Genghiz Khan had chosen ages before as the site of his grave, not far from the region of his birth in the headwaters of the Onon River. But no one knows where his remains lie. A herd of horses was driven backwards and forwards over the ground after the burial in order to conceal all traces of the spot, and within a few years the weather and natural regeneration had made it indistinguishable from the surrounding emptiness. But not before forty maidens from the most distinguished families in Mongolia had been sacrificed there, together with a number of prized horses the khan might also have need of in his Eternal Heaven.

The empire continued to expand under Ogodei, who gave it a capital in the walled settlement of Karakorum, though this fell into decay within forty years, after the centre of gravity shifted to a restored Peking. Installed as Great Khan in 1229, Ogodei saw his eastern armies crossing the Yalu River in Korea within a couple of years, and the oriental campaign preoccupied the Mongol hordes until the Koreans were almost pacified and the Chinese further contained. There was then a brilliantly swift winter invasion of northern Russia across frozen rivers and the more leisurely mopping up of one princedom after another until, by 1240, the land was totally subjugated. That same year, the Mongol armies launched a double attack to the west, on Poland and Hungary, where they proved themselves as irresistible as they had been everywhere before. Twelve months later they had crossed the Danube, still heading west, and they got as far as Neustadt, just below Vienna, before a halt was called in 1242. And what stopped them was no army that any Europeans could muster, but news from Mongolia that Ogodei had died, that a quriltai of the Mongol leaders had been summoned to choose a new khan.

So the stench of these invaders drifted slowly back across the Carpathians; never to return so far west, as it happened, though this was by no means the end of the Mongol Empire. There were other khans and generals waiting to shape its future, most notably four grandsons of Genghiz Khan. Two of these were merely outstanding commanders: Batu, who led the Golden Horde in its conquest of Russia and laid the foundations of an imperium there that lasted almost two hundred and fifty years; and Hulegu, who destroyed the Assassins before smashing his way into Baghdad and forcing Aleppo and Damascus to capitulate. Two others succeeded to the highest leadership: Mongke Khan followed by Kublai Khan, under whom the armies campaigned as far south as Burma and the Indian Deccan, as far east as Japan and, in the quadrant between, as distantly as Java. The Japanese successfully resisted the invaders through their superiority in warfare at sea, but only once were the Mongols ever defeated during this period in a battle on land: when, in 1260, near the village of Nazareth in Palestine, an Egyptian Mameluke army used its numerical superiority to put Hulegu's tumens into unfeigned retreat. What finished the empire was partly the inertia, the lack of will to take the strain any longer, that overcomes all imperialisms in the end; and partly the mounting aggression of the Islamic warlord Timur, who the English-speaking also know as Tamburlaine.

The story of the Mongol expansion, with its blood-letting, destruction and pillage would be numbingly rebarbative were it not for consequences that had never before followed such human savagery. For although Genghiz Khan and his heirs could exterminate entire communities without the slightest hesitation, and although they exacted full tribute from all the lands they controlled by threat of arms, the harshness of their authority was generally tempered by an unusual tolerance of local custom. The shrewdness that adopted Chinese siege warfare for greater fighting efficiency, and enlisted the Uighurs to remedy the inherent illiteracy of the Mongols, also ensured that the conquered lands were left in a fit condition to yield the required tribute and to serve other Mongol purposes. The laws which the Chinese, the Persians, the Russians and others had evolved in the past remained in force with the permission of the overlords, though it was understood that they must not infringe the Yasa, the accretion of Mongol custom and ordinance which Genghiz Khan codified the moment he had the Uighurs to transcribe it from the verbal sources. Even more remarkably, the Mongols never attempted to proselytise those they subdued. They might demolish Christian churches, reduce Taoist shrines, burn the mosques of Islam in the course of their siege warfare, but the survivors – if there were any – were at liberty to pick up the pieces and worship as before once the warfare was done. Church-building in Russia came to a standstill for a century as a result of the Mongol invasion, yet what was left of the Orthodox Church after 1240 retained all its old influence and eventually became exceedingly rich. Its taxation was waived in return for offering continuous prayer on behalf of the khan and his family, and it also profited from the international commerce that flourished under the Mongolian peace.

There are several credible witnesses to the substance of that peace, among them Marco Polo, who may or may not have held an appointment under Kublai Khan, but certainly spent twenty years in his domain. At different times earlier in the thirteenth century there were two Franciscan friars. It is to John of Plano Carpini, who was the Pope's envoy to the Great Khan, that we owe our detailed knowledge of the Mongol armies, their equipment and their tactics, for he was a meticulous observer of many irreligious things. William of Rubruck, who had similar credentials from King Louis IX of France in the decade after John's embassy, visited the Mongol capital of Karakorum in 1254 and reported that "not counting the Khan's palace it is not as large as the village of St Denis, and the monastery of St Denis is worth ten times more than that palace".

What these and other European travellers remark on time and again is the efficiency of the Mongol administrators, wherever they went, the discipline of every Mongol they encountered, whatever his task, and the total safety that was guaranteed to anyone making a journey wherever the khan's authority ran. All three characteristics are exemplified in accounts we have of the Yam, the mounted courier service that Genghiz Khan started in 1206, which is said to have been the fastest communications system the world ever knew until modern technology was devised. It originated in the warlord's insistence on up-to-date information from all his commanders in the field before he ordered the next move, and it functioned superbly from the very beginning because of symbiosis between every Mongol and his horse. The couriers rode relays of horses for hours at a time, ringing a bell as they approached the post where the next mount was saddled up and ready to go, covering great distances at phenomenal speeds similar to those that had made them such devastating cavalry in war. Some were capable of riding well over a thousand miles with a message, on very little rest at the staging posts. So much did the Yam become the pride of the Mongol Empire that foreign ambassadors were encouraged to use it for diplomatic purposes, and even merchants were allowed to avail themselves of its services, which did something to encourage long-distance trade.

Yet the benefits of the Pax Mongolica were not what struck me most of all the day I stood contemplating the desolation that had been Merv before Genghiz Khan's youngest son passed that way. As I gazed across the barren brown plain of the Turkmen, it seemed to me that pictures of Hiroshima after the atom bomb did not more clearly illustrate what happens when a place is razed to the ground. Evgeni, who had himself been the child of despoliation in war, looked around blankly, appearing to be bored by the lack of spectacle, by the dusty drabness that was oppressive in its uneventfulness. He gestured with a sweep of his arm that needed no words to amplify its complaint.

"But there is nothing to see here," he said. "This is, I think, a grave disappointment to you." He shook his head testily, as though the arrangements had failed in some way that pained him on my behalf.

Merv was not at all a disappointment to me; its very extinction was fascinating. That such a metropolis could be obliterated without explosives was a form of ingenuity, a brutal audacity. It also raised questions about the influence, the nature, the course, the origins of evil. What was Genghiz Khan's legacy to the world apart from providing a model for the Pony Express, and perhaps showing the imperial British how to rule India with a certain amount of acumen? Could the courier service, the safe travel, the tolerance of alien religions even mitigate, let alone excuse, the butchery, the violation and the wreckage that preceded them and sometimes made them possible? Was I to stand appalled before the ruins of Merv and the memory of its dead, or must I dismiss it with a sad shrug because this was no more than the way of the world seven hundred years ago?

I could resolve most of these questions at least enough to quieten my concern. Yet one other continued to engage me as the woman from the museum drove us away from that derelict place, back to the bleak nullity of modern Mary. I believed I could understand well enough how and why the Mongol Empire eventually expired, but what force had been responsible for begetting it? Why would a nomad people who inhabited one of the greatest voids on earth and had no need of extra space, who later returned to the restless mode of their ancestors, with its limited territorial ambitions . . . why would they suddenly decide to annexe the whole of creation if that could be done? Was it simply in obedience to the urge of one man who, bereft of father as a boy and betrayed by his clan, had sworn to revenge himself upon the world?

5

The Crescent and the Star

The fourth city of the Soviet Union satisfied a trivial but long-standing curiosity of mine. One of my insignificant childhood memories was of the wireless (as we called it in those days) in the house of my grandparents, a rotund appliance encased in an unattractive substance known as Bakelite, a brittle synthetic which in this instance had been manufactured in the colour referred to quite innocently by my elders as nigger brown. There was a sizeable aperture in its shiny surface, covered by a piece of cloth which concealed the loudspeaker, and below this was a smaller opening in the case, containing the dial and a red pointer that moved across it when you twiddled a knob. A series of baffling numbers were marked on the dial, as were some words which appealed to me much more: Droitwich, Luxembourg,

Hilversum – and Tashkent. The first three I not only located in an atlas but even managed to obtain signals from, though these were sometimes unintelligible. Although I found Tashkent on the map, too, I'm not sure I was clear which country it was in, and I do not recall ever having heard anything that might have been broadcast from there. Even now I cannot imagine why a council house in pre-war Lancashire should notionally have been able to tune in to what was still often thought of as Russian Turkestan. At the age of seven or eight I merely rolled Tashkent around my imagination, murmured its alien name to myself, and wondered whether I would ever see it one day.

The city which I eventually reached in the depths of its winter sprawled extensively between the desert and the steppe. Though it was bitterly cold there was little snow about, but thick mud awaited the pedestrian almost every-where, once the main streets were left behind. It was es-pecially adhesive in the barren spaces that separated the endless housing blocks of the suburbs, and in the meander-ing lanes of the old quarter, which survived from the time when there was a considerable slave market here. Few of the old houses remained, partly because the city soviet was bent on modernisation and had condemned buildings of that period as insanitary, but also because most of the mud-walled dwellings had collapsed in the 1966 earthquake, when one-third of Tashkent was destroyed. Given that this was a notoriously unstable area which had already suffered disaster, I didn't expect to find that the city's great pride nowadays was an expanding subway system modelled extra-vagantly on Moscow's. In one station the walls were lavishly decorated with mosaic, in the next station bronze sculpture was the motif, and at the stop after that chandeliers dangled sparkling from the tunnel roof. The trains ran as swiftly as any I have known, a taped message announced the stops in plenty of time for the passengers to pick them out, and the doors opened and closed to a melodious chime: but whenever I travelled underground, the compartments were just as crowded as at rush hour on the Piccadilly Line.

On the surface, the citizens commuted in electric tram-cars and in the red and cream buses which seem to do service throughout the communist world, here bearing gas cylinders the size of torpedoes on their roofs. They trundled along in convoy with cumbersome lorries belching sulphurous fumes that would presently join the muck emitted by factories which made Tashkent vital to the national economy. Only Moscow, Leningrad and Kiev were more significant. This was a very big base of heavy industry; including, someone told me almost in a whisper, an important part of Soviet aircraft production. Perhaps as a result of replanning after the earthquake, the traffic travelled out of the city centre along extremely wide roads which could take three vehicles abreast in each direction quite easily. Except in that small area of old lanes, the entire city was an overwhelming rejection of all that was traditional in the urban life of Asia, especially the closeness of buildings, the limited view from the front door, the acute sense of neighbourhood. Everything here was spacious, with large perspectives and a feeling that you might never get to know the people in the next building except in time of general catastrophe. Tashkent was not a place for agoraphobes, who might jib at crossing the average boulevard and be petrified at the prospect of the smallest civic park. In one of these was a monument to the earthquake, in which a family stood defiant as the ground opened up before them. At their feet, set into a marble cube, was a clockface announcing the moment, 5.22, when the frightful upheaval occurred.

By the time I had walked some distance on my first exploration of the city centre, I was quite ready for the revelation that here was the biggest square in the Soviet Union. It was two or three times the size of Red Square in Moscow, large enough to accommodate a couple of villages, and from any point on its perimeter it was only just possible to make out figures moving along the opposite edge across an expanse of tarmac and cobblestones. It was, of course, dedicated to Lenin; and although it was so vast that nothing short of the Eiffel Tower could possibly have dominated it, someone had made the attempt by erecting half-way down one side the nation's largest statue of the demi-god. An enormous base of red granite had been imposed upon the square in a succession of terraces, with a flight of steps so wide that a regiment might have marched up them in order to stand at ease around more red granite, which rose much higher in a colossal pedestal. On this was the figure in bronze, his bald pate, I estimated, about as far from the ground as the torch held by the Statue of Liberty. The head, gazing steadfastly at a distant horizon somewhere far beyond the municipal boundaries of Tashkent, was very stern and unblinking.

It looked even more like Lenin than the real thing, which I had queued to see the first time I visited Moscow. With hundreds of others, I had been held back by the militia on the slope above the Alexander Gardens until the clock on the Spassky Tower struck eleven and we were allowed to approach the blockhouse under the Kremlin wall, where the day's reverence began. Two at a time we entered the grey marbled tomb and carefully descended a few steps, while people cleared their throats and got rid of their coughs, just as they do before curtain-up. Abruptly we turned into a gloomy cavern, with an almost phosphorescent glow in the middle. And there he was. Lenin was ringed by perhaps a dozen soldiers, who were not in position for a lying-in-state. They had their backs to him, true, but they did not stand in mourning, looking at the floor. They were watching every move that anybody made in that tomb. It would have taken courage to reach for a handkerchief. It would also have taken willpower for me to shift my gaze from that immortal corpse.

The glow was theatrically orange, and for the eternal minute or so that everyone was permitted in the presence of Lenin, there was nothing in the world but that large head with its close-cut ginger beard and its flaring nostrils; and those two hands lying straight and apart. I was never nearer than maybe ten feet from him, so that what I was seeing could have been mummified tissue, which is the authorised

104

truth; or it could have been wax or plastic which had been moulded into the image of a man, what the iconoclasts believe. I could not tell whether the orange light was coming from a canopy or the ceiling or from some other source. I wasn't even aware of legs or a torso; just that mesmerising head, and two hands with the first finger on the right one slightly crooked, all garishly spotlit upon a jet-black cloth. And soldiers with flickering eyes. And people moving ahead of me and behind me like a force of destiny. They had been very quiet as they approached the tomb. They were even quieter as they walked out into the Kremlin gardens, past the lesser interments just inside the crenellated wall.

On this journey through Central Asia I had, in a small way, become a student of Lenin statues, casually savouring the difference between one and another. Here in Tashkent was Lenin *maximus*, standing firmly with his feet well apart, which was no more than common sense in such a windy position. He wore a long and thick coat, which was also wise at such an altitude. His left arm was close to his side but the other was offering a document portentously enough for it to have been a treaty or a manifesto, though at that height above eye-level it could equally have been a rolled-up newspaper. Standing in his shadow, I remembered the Lenin *parvus* (conceivably *minimus*) I had encountered in the middle of the steppe, standing on his little plinth in the small village square, also well coated against the elements, and amiably giving the thumbs-up to those versatile Kazakh maidens who were about to take part in the beauty contest. Not that Kazakhstan invariably restricted itself to figures as diminutive as that. There was a towering Lenin in Semipalatinsk, fumbling at his watch-chain with one hand and gesturing with the other in the general direction of the Soviet nuclear-testing site not so very far away, which may have been the reason why the pedestal in this case was not raised too far off the ground, in order to minimise the effect of subterranean fission and consequent disturbance in the open air. In Frunze a goodly-sized Lenin had opened his coat and his jacket to reveal the waistcoat

105

underneath, while an outstretched arm pointed to visions that may not yet have been evident to the commonalty of Kirghizia. In Dushanbe, his copy of that morning's *Pravda* was more discreetly held, and he seemed to be emphasising that he had nothing up his other sleeve. Meanwhile, the good Turkmen of Ashkhabad beheld him on an elaborate superstructure decorated in dazzlingly multi-coloured tiles, his head cocked slightly on one side as though he was straining to catch the faintest sound, perhaps of a time bomb ticking away just across the border in Iran.

A suspicion was forming in my mind that no two Lenins in the Soviet Union were quite alike; which, if true, would mean that in this as in no other choices laid before them, the proletariat enjoyed a variety that put them on almost level terms with the nomenklatura. Perhaps I had unwittingly stumbled on a pattern among these options, in which the pose, the semblance of the man, was most carefully related to the site where each statue would finish up: as with the outstretched arm commanding the nuclear physicists of Semipalatinsk, the thumbs-up in the middle of the Kazakh steppe (the beauty contest was presumably an annual event, hence the need for perpetual encouragement), the hearkening ear close to the Iranian border in Turkmenia, the resolute stance on the windswept plateau in Tashkent.

If this were so, then there must surely be a Lenin somewhere along the Volga, straining in exemplary fashion to haul up an anchor, or maybe standing Olympically in oarsman's singlet and shorts with one fist firmly clasping the blade from a racing shell. Might there not then be a version on the banks of the Don, in schizophrenic Kletsko-Potchtovsky maybe, or riparian Rossosh, or in blunt Boguchar, where Lenin could be admired as an exponent of the Cossack dance, with silver bullets emblazoning his lapels in the manner of the late Nelson Eddy? Nothing too abandoned, of course, just a little knees-bend. Something more thoughtful would be appropriate in Kiev, both because it lay at the heart of the potentially dissident Ukraine and because it had ever been a centre of Orthodoxy, so that here

106

the palms of the hands might be slyly together, which the Christians could mistake for prayer, and the apparatchiki for the birthpangs of the dialectic. From Kiev no more than a few hundred versts would separate Lenin from the western frontier of the state he had begotten, which would make Brest–Litovsk, overlooking the Bug and its multitude of carp fishermen, where he had once been humiliated in making a peace treaty with Germany, an appropriate spot for him to raise his fingers delicately at the sun setting over European capitalism.

He would be unwise to risk a similar salute in the direction of the Americans or the Japanese from his eastern extremities, unless he did it cautiously from the Kamchatskaya Oblast or from Sakhalin, or from some other position safely below 66° 32′ North. Above that latitude the Arctic temperatures are at certain times of the year so abysmally low that the digits of even a brazen Lenin would be at risk, made so brittle by the perishing cold that they would be liable to drop off and vanish into some deep drift of snow, which would only encourage the capitalists. In all such areas, indeed, Lenin would be well advised to expose himself to the elements only in a pair of gloves, if not thermo-nuclear underwear as well. Thus clad he could face the rigours of Siberia with some confidence, waving to foreign tourists from station platforms on its celebrated railway, urging to greater efforts the Stakhanovite foresters of the taiga, reproving penal colonists amid the frozen marshes of the tundra. In Irkutsk it would be politic to wear a mink coat with accessories, out of deference to the local fur trade, and in Novosibirsk he would have to make up his mind whether he was going to hail the steel workers in a hard hat, or whether he would posture like Canute to express solidarity with the scientists of Akademgorodok, in their efforts to reverse the flow of Siberian rivers, so that these will empty themselves fruitfully into Central Asia rather than so wastefully into the Barents Sea.

It had occurred to me that there might be more than one pattern in the graven imagery of Lenin. I had merely come across the topographical form, but there could well be another that had so far eluded me, a biographical theme that fixed as artistically as possible his life and times, from the birth in 1870 to the resurrection soon after 1924. Perhaps – dare one entertain such a hope? – in some provincial town (how perfect it would be if this were Simbirsk, on the Volga, where Vladimir Ilyich Ulyanov began) he was remembered not as the bearded figure who shook John Reed in October 1917, but as the lad who was yet to be the superman; in which case a modest figurine would suffice, wearing around its neck and above its first waistcoat the cross that was thrown away forever at the age of fifteen. A full-scale statue, but certainly no more than life-size, would depict him at leisure a few years later, wondering what to do with the pawn in his hand, or possibly executing an arabesque while skimming across thin ice, for both chess and skating were among his accomplishments. Some collective in the Soviet breadbasket might well have a Lenin cast as a tractor driver or a rural mechanic, in memory of his farming time after expulsion from the University of Kazan. That was for political activity, when he composed improper messages in potassium bichromate and other sorts of invisible ink: and what a challenge to any sculptor, rendering that period of Lenin's life in bronze would be. Much easier to convey his habit of doing fifty press-ups to keep warm in his prison cell, or of swatting away from his face the mosquitoes that plagued him during the three summers he spent in exile at Shushenskoye, which would have been penance enough without his self-imposed task of translating Sidney and Beatrice Webb as well.

It may have been during this first of his many exiles that Lenin developed his theory of dialectical subterfuge, which he employed at various times after that when he was slipping in and out of the country. After the London Congress in 1907 he travelled to Finland cleanshaven and wearing a broad straw hat, so as to deflect any pursuit by the Metropolitan Police. There must surely be a statuesque version of this, though admittedly it might be hard to recognise. He spent a great deal of 1917 in disguise, and it is unthinkable

108

that art would have neglected to record it in metal or stone. When Kerensky formed his government in July, Lenin fled to Finland disguised as a railway fireman. A few weeks later he returned to Petrograd for a nocturnal meeting in Sukharov's flat, wearing a wig, and abruptly went into hiding again at three in the morning, perhaps with the wig askew. In November he arrived at the Smolny Institute unrecognised by the Bolsheviks guarding the door; and no wonder, when he'd swathed his face in a bandage so that no one who saw him on the way would know who he was. One might spend a thoroughly absorbing holiday with the co-operation of Intourist, tracking down three such collector's pieces as those: Lenin as engine-driver's mate, Lenin looking like the central figure in a bad accident, Lenin in drag. I could think of one other statue that would perfectly complement that trio. In this piece Lenin would stand confidently, exuding gravitas, his left hand grasping the lapel of his jacket as men of affairs often do, but his other hand would hang loose behind him, and it would be cupped. Donations to party funds invariably meant maintaining Lenin's solvency first.

The question was, when and where had Lenin modelled for these effusions? They must be counted in thousands, for the Soviet town or village without its statue of Lenin is unthinkable, the bigger cities boasting them in multiples. He is much, much more numerous than even Queen Victoria used to be throughout the British Empire and she came in only two poses, the sitting and the standing up, always with an orb and sceptre in her hands, which left no scope at all for artistic imagination, let alone licence; whereas I envisaged the permutations of Lenin as nearly infinite as those in a football pool. Lenin, moreover, was an extremely busy fellow, even when he wasn't messing about with potassium bichromate and dithering over which wig to wear today. Given the variations which it seemed reasonable to postulate from the limited evidence of my own eyes, and the time any self-respecting sculptor would require of his subject so that he could get the proportions of the body, the

109

character of the individual, the mood to be conveyed exactly right, it must have cost the great man weeks, if not months, of his life every year in sitting or standing for the artists eager to memorialise him. And that would have been the case if only one sculptor had been involved in the creation of each statue. But sometimes they came in teams, as they did when producing the statue at Frunze, which was the work – according to a postcard in my possession – of sculptors A. Kibalnikov, T. Sadyakov and V. Protkov, not to mention a brace of architects as well. Each would demand his meed of time in discussing matters with the subject first, and the wonder is that when actually on the job they didn't get in each other's way. Perhaps they did, as medical men sometimes do when performing cardio-vascular by-pass surgery, where one is opening up the leg to withdraw the surplus vessels, while his colleague-in-chief is delving into the chest to prepare for the new grafts (God knows what the third sculptor might be up to while the other two were similarly engaged on Lenin's bronze). How, then, did Lenin manage to accommodate this long procession of importunates who wished to perpetuate him in effigy?

The tentative answer I had begun to formulate was that the modelling might have been related to the periods when Lenin was apparently in exile. Perhaps he never was in exile, in the accepted political sense. Perhaps those years in Switzerland were not after all spent in plotting the Russian Revolution with Krupskaya, but in clandestinely posing for the sculptors. He would not wish to be found doing this at home, obviously, because there is such a thing as professional jealousy among revolutionaries, as there is with any other trade, and nobody was asking Trotsky, Axelrod, Molotov, Sokolov, Sukhanov, Steklov, Zalutski and the other Bolsheviks to stand for their statues. I could see very well how the arrangements would run. Lenin would go disguised to the Finland Station and catch a train to almost anywhere – he always travelled into and returned from 'exile' through Petrograd, remember – and some time later, after he had reached his destination and sent a message back

110

in invisible ink, a sculptor would take himself down to the Smolensk Station, or some other Moscow railway terminus, and set off incognito and circuitously for the rendezvous. No third party could possibly perceive a connection between the two journeys. If my theory was correct, it might explain a small lacuna in the hagiography. On April 9th, 1917, Lenin prepared to return home from Switzerland, and with some friends had a farewell lunch at the Zahringer Hof in Zurich. Either there or just before the train pulled out (accounts vary on this point) there was an argument with a man named Oscar Blum, which ended with Lenin taking him by the scruff of the neck and kicking him out of the room (or compartment). There was some suspicion that Blum was an agent of the Okhrana, though this has never been proved. It is quite likely that he was no such thing. It is not impossible that he was a sculptor who had just finished a maquette as a preliminary to casting the statue itself, and that this so displeased its subject that Lenin became possessed of an intemperate rage.

One question remained, and it was the weightiest of them all. Supposing the Soviet authorities decided it would be healthier if the cult of Lenin were brought to an end, as the veneration of Stalin finished one unsuspecting day. What would happen to all these statues? People could hardly be expected to ignore the man when he stood there, on a prime site in the middle of every town, eye-balling each passer-by from dawn to dusk and through to the next breakfast-time. This country had enough troubles already without adding a nationwide epidemic of hemeralopia to them. There would have to be the greatest dismantling operation the USSR had ever known, far surpassing the demolition of the Romanovs, a levelling for which the reduction of Stalin, it would be seen, was merely a practice run. Throughout the fifteen republics, brigades of special activists would be formed, each led by a putative Hero of Soviet Labour, with apple-cheeked young people in red kerchiefs to the fore, all eager to fulfil their duty in the class struggle to knock Lenin off his pedestals at last. On

111

an appointed night they would move into every community with their jack-hammers and their saws, their
crowbars and their drills, their winches and their haulage
gear, and the hours of darkness from one end of this
empire to the other, from Severnaya Zemlya to the
Caspian, from Vladivostok to Chop, would ring to the
sound of statues being brought low.

Transport of every kind would have been commandeered
meanwhile, in order to dispose of all the scrap metal, and
by morning it would be on the move. Normal services on
the trans-Siberian railway would probably be suspended for
twenty-four hours, while tens of thousands of tons of Lenin
were passed along. Other portions of his anatomies would
be conveyed here and there by trucks. Very small statues
in outlying settlements could be brought to railheads by
tarantass or, where conditions demanded it, by horse-drawn
sledges driven by fur-coated men cracking long whips across
the snowfields. Steamers might have to be requisitioned
into leaving room for manifestations of Lenin on voyages
over the inland seas. But demonstrations while these con-
signments traversed the eleven time zones of the nation
would be discouraged, so there would be no overt reaction
from the population as the arms and legs and bald heads and
goatee beards passed by in all their bronzed and infinite
variety. Instead, for the first time, sublimely unaware Young
Octobrists would enjoy merely infantile things in their
classrooms that day, and their older siblings in the Komso-
mol would no longer take life quite so seriously. Bureaucrats
spread thickly across the oblasts would cudgel their wits to
determine whether a Marxist made any sense without being
propped up by a hyphenated Leninist, and the rank and file
of party members would be acknowledging that the time
had come to hand in their cards.

Most people, in fact, would simply ask themselves what
on earth the Central Committee was going to do with all
the bronze that had come to it in such an unprecedented
windfall. That decision would have been taken already in
closed session, one of the Soviet Union's few remaining

state secrets. There would be such a quantity by the time it was all stockpiled, that an obvious solution would be to recycle it through the blast furnaces of Magnitogorsk, the Bessemer converters of the Donets, and other arcanely ferrous processes. But the USSR's economy had for too long been in hock to heavy industry, and the chances are that some smart young chap in Soyuzmetallurgprom would come up with something much more subtle than that. He would propose a flotation of Lenin on the international commodities market, to produce such a glut of alloy that there would be repercussions of profound significance all over the world. Copper prices in Zambia would be thrown into disarray, and so would tin-mining in the Cordillera of Bolivia. Futures in zinc and lead would be affected, which would produce ribellione on the streets of Sardinia and stoush in the pubs of Broken Hill. The biggest impact of all, however, would be at Comex in New York City, the world's most important metal exchange, where the brokers and the speculators would go bananas as Lenin came floating past. The whole Western economy could well be affected. It was not beyond the bounds of possibility – and here the young thruster from Nogina Square would have a wicked gleam in his eye – that Vladimir Ilyich might precipitate another, and this time conclusive, Wall Street Crash; something he had never managed to provoke in his lifetime. This would be the ultimate triumph of Marxism–Leninism even if, by then, almost every Soviet citizen was at long last looking the other way.

I should have liked Evgeni's opinion of this scenario, but we had parted on reaching Tashkent. He had announced some days before that it would be necessary for him to return to Moscow, where he would see me again before I went home. The reason for his withdrawal, he said, was that his office staff were becoming mutinous at his continued absence. He had regularly phoned the capital, I knew, to inform them of our progress two thousand miles away, though sometimes it had taken several hours for the call to get through.

113

"Also," he added, "it is high time I was keeping an eye on my domestics again." This puzzled me at first, because I had not thought Evgeni sufficiently senior in the hierarchy to be provided with servants; but he was referring to his wife and his unmarried daughter, who lived with her parents in a three-roomed flat.

His replacement was awaiting us when we arrived from Merv and Ashkhabad, a mere boy, I thought, when I first set eyes on him, though Vladik was ten years older than he looked, a husband and father of two. Everything about him suggested the college student, and his laughter had the unaffected joy of youth. One could hardly expect him to equal Evgeni's total command of English, which resulted from a lifetime's wide reading and listening. He also lacked the older man's self-assurance, and this became apparent very soon after we were introduced.

Moscow's planning of the expedition had meant that everywhere I and my companion travelled, there was a local contact to whom we could turn at once for any assistance we required. He would arrange meetings, fix transport, solve small but irritating problems, see us safely installed in lodgings; attend, in short, to all the trifling matters that consume so much of the traveller's time and energy in a strange place. Sometimes the he was a she, most notably Usmanova in Kazakhstan, and not once had anyone failed Evgeni and me – except, perhaps, in not trying hard enough to reach the Stone Tower, though in that case I was obviously expecting too much. I had never been so comprehensively taken care of before, in journeys I had made all over the world.

The contact in Tashkent was one Barak, a native of the city who almost certainly had never ventured outside Uzbekistan. He was a stocky fellow in his thirties, paler than most Uzbeks and with a broader nose than some, but with the local characteristic of black hair and dark eyes. In my company he was always dressed in a smart overcoat and an astrakhan hat, and I rarely saw him without his hands in his pockets except when driving his car. His eyes glanced

114

everywhere but at your face when you were talking to him, and his speech was not much more than a mutter, as though it was too much trouble to make the effort to be heard. At first I thought he might be a slightly dense man, congenitally lazier than most, although nothing more difficult to deal with than that. But then, shortly after having said goodbye to Evgeni, I came down from my room in the hotel to meet Vladik in the lobby, as we had arranged half an hour earlier. Vladik was at the reception desk, in conversation with one of the staff. Barak was standing almost hidden behind a pillar just inside the hotel entrance, and did not see me coming down the stairs. His eyes never left the fair-haired young Russian a dozen yards away, and I was startled by the expression on his face. It was something between a sneer and fundamental anger, an utterly venomous glare.

I went up to the desk and leaned alongside Vladik. "How's it going?" I asked.

He smiled, a little tightly, I thought. "Oh, it's OK. Just one or two things to sort out with passports and travel documents."

"I thought our friend was supposed to deal with all that." I jerked my head in the direction of the pillar, so that Vladik turned and noticed him for the first time. Barak was still steadily watching, but his face had softened into a sneer alone. He made not the slightest sign of recognition.

Vladik's smile tightened a little more. "I think the office forgot to brief me properly. I think I didn't bring enough presents." He laughed, but he was not amused.

Ah, so that was it. Barak's palm had not been greased in the manner to which he was accustomed. Well, he belonged to a republic of legendary corruption, where backhanders were the normal currency of getting through each day, and where some rip-offs were of a magnitude that staggered other Soviet citizens, cynical as they all were about most forms of public behaviour. Bribery had a long history in Uzbekistan, but it had become notoriously worse under the patronage of Leonid Brezhnev, whose rise in the communist ranks owed much the fact that here, second only to

115

Kazakhstan, had been his power base ever since he was made first secretary to the party at Alma-Ata in 1954. When, ten years later, he was securely in the Kremlin, his former associates and placemen in Uzbekistan began to reap the rewards of assiduous toadying. The Uzbek party chief, Sharaf Rashidov, built no fewer than thirty mansions out of state funds in order to provide hospitality for Brezhnev, his family and his entourage whenever they chose to revisit Central Asia. Subsequently these were disposed of for up to £1 million apiece, money that went straight into Rashidov's pocket. Mrs Yadegar Nassreddinova, who held various senior posts in the Tashkent administration, had also built for private profit out of the public purse and had spent more than £100,000 of the state's money on her son's wedding.

An Uzbek Mafia had fattened themselves in various criminal ways, including the embezzlement of more than £5,000 million in fifteen years; most commonly by falsifying official records of cotton production – Uzbekistan's biggest industry – and diverting raw materials and finished textiles onto the black market. All these matters had come to light after Brezhnev's death, as a result of preliminary investigations ordered by Yuri Andropov. But they had not become public knowledge until Gorbachev authorised it. There had been trials, there had been suicides, there had been executions, there had been imprisonments, as one big fish after another was identified; including Brezhnev's son-in-law Yuri Churbanov, who had accepted £700,000 in cash from Rashidov. But some members of the Mafia had come through the investigations intact and were still living in some style, with homes in both Moscow and Tashkent. And no one doubted that Uzbekistan remained essentially what it had always been, the sewer of the USSR.

"Look," I said, "I've got one or two goodies left in my bag upstairs that I brought out from England. I'll go and find something that might cheer him up a bit."

Vladik shook his head and pulled a face. "Thanks, but I think you'll be wasting them on him."

"But you shouldn't have to mess around with this sort of

116

thing. It's his job. He should have done it the moment we walked in here. That's what your people pay him for. If we let him freewheel now, he'll take a holiday all week."

"It's not worth it. It'll make too many waves." He shrugged and his shoulders were resigned.

Barak had a glitter in his eye when we joined him by the door, but it was not a friendly one. He led the way down the long cascade of steps from the hotel to the level of the street, hands still deep in his coat pockets. When we reached the pavement, he nodded towards a subway entrance a few yards away.

"You get the Metro down there," he muttered. "It'll take you where you're going. I have to be back in the office. If you need me again, you can ring me there."

He walked away in the opposite direction, towards his car, without another word. I gaped, and Vladik laughed at my astonishment. I had come across no one nearly as boorish as this man in a long while, but my companion remained remarkably cool about it. "Don't let it get to you," he said. "We're used to it. It happens all the time down here."

It happened the next day, in fact, much more pointedly. I came down to the lobby again and this time the two were standing together. Vladik looked pale and cornered as he listened to an animated monologue that Barak was pouring into his right ear. I greeted them, but Vladik only looked up briefly and raised his eyebrows. The Uzbek's acknowledgment was to shift his stance slightly, so that his back was more completely between me and his face. He was speaking so rapidly in his thick accent that in the rush of sibilants I caught almost nothing but the words "you people think . . . " He was emphasising certain things by raising his head slightly each time in a jerk. A Berber I had once travelled with in the Sahara used to make the same gesture when wishing to indicate that something had happened 'over there', pointing with his forehead instead of with his hands. I had noticed it in different circumstances since; invariably among Muslims. Other people had their own body language, but that signal was peculiar to Islam. A

117

penny suddenly dropped. When Barak turned and stumped out of the building, with a curt nod to me as he passed, I watched him go and then said to my companion, " 'You people' meaning 'You Russians,' I take it."

"That's right. We're the wicked imperialists, didn't you know?" Vladik's face brightened, and he grinned again, mockingly.

His failure to come to Tashkent with lavish gifts had triggered a much deeper grudge in the Uzbek. The venom I had noticed in Barak's stare earlier stemmed from a long cultural hostility which had reached a local peak when General Chernyayev and his troops captured the city in the nineteenth century and declared it part of Alexander II's Russia. All over Central Asia, Russian generals were then rolling back the frontiers of Islam; but this was merely the latest episode in a mutual animosity which went back to the greatest of all Russian traumas, the Mongol invasion resulting in those two medieval centuries of the Tatarchina, the Tartar Yoke. The Golden Horde commanded by Genghiz Khan's grandson Batu was still inclined to shamanism when it reached Kiev in 1240, but before the thirteenth century was out a majority of Mongols had converted to Islam – a rare example of conquerors adopting the religion of their vassals – so that in the Christian Russian mind the long Mongol occupation of their country was eventually translated into the Aziachina, the Asian Yoke. The Golden Horde had in time divided itself into three khanates, the biggest of them centred on the city of Kazan on the Volga. And it was at Muslim Kazan that the Russians took their first dreadful revenge for the humiliation they had suffered under the yoke of the Mongols, the Tartars, the Asians.

The yoke had been lifted in 1480, when Ivan III stopped paying tribute to the alien authority, by then too vitiated to enforce it. The revenge was taken by his grandson Ivan the Terrible, first Tsar of all Russia, first Tsar to raise the old Byzantine standard of the double-headed eagle, a ruler who saw himself in direct line of succession to both St Peter and the Emperor Constantine. In 1550 he led his armies on a holy war against the infidel in Kazan, by then a city of over 100,000 with 150 mosques. He brought cannon to breach its walls and his troops poured into the outer districts, where they slaughtered thousands and took many slaves before withdrawing because they were unable to break into the more heavily fortified citadel in the centre of Kazan. Two years later Ivan was back with a larger force and more gunpowder. The city was mined and blown apart in the biggest explosion human beings had yet contrived. Some 50,000 Muslims perished this time, and every living young woman was taken as a concubine. The mosques and the madrassas were destroyed, their clerics were killed. Survivors were invited to choose between baptism and death. Some escaped both fates and fled into exile. And although the martyrdom of Kazan had always been dismissed by the Christians as a just punishment, Islam had never let the more grievous memory go. It had festered quietly ever since, while other injuries and insults were periodically added to the original offence.

Peter the Great's decision to push south in the eighteenth century began the subjugation of Central Asia, which had almost wholly been Russified within 150 years. Russian armies moved on the Muslims of the Caucasus too, but there the local hill fighters held them off for decades in a bitter guerrilla war. There was no such possibility on the flatness of the steppe, which was perfectly suited to the dominance of the big military expedition. Local defence forces, in any case, were uncoordinated. By the nineteenth century there was such a long history of internecine warfare between the emirs, the sultans and the khans that there was no chance of unity against the invader. The one cry that might have brought cohesion – Jihad! – was out of the question because the rulers were not only corrupt and cruel, but openly lax in their religious observances. Their people mostly loathed them, and were disinclined to die in a holy war drummed up for the convenience of such men.

So the Russians came south and did not deal gently with the local populations who obstructed them. General

Kauffmann, who became Alexander's viceroy in Central Asia with his headquarters in Tashkent, put down a local Uzbek revolt brutally, deported hundreds to Siberia, redistributed their lands among Slav settlers, and introduced a new form of punishment by blowing up the homes of anyone suspected of a leading role in the rising. At the same time, Muslims in what had now become Russian Turkestan were allowed certain freedoms later denied them by the Bolsheviks, provided they submitted to the ultimate authority of the Tsar. They were not cut off by frontier restrictions from their co-religionists in adjacent lands, which was important to a people whose instincts were still nomadic, with wide affinities elsewhere. Uzbeks in Russian Turkestan had powerful loyalties which they shared with Pathans in British India, and were still able to exercise. Nor did the Tsars press them into serving with the imperial army, though the reasons were less than generous: they didn't think much of Muslims as fighters, and preferred not to teach them the use of modern weapons.

Changing this policy during the Great War produced a bloody rebellion. Hard-pressed in the European conflict, the Russians conscripted 250,000 Muslims, but told them that they were not required to go into battle, merely to dig trenches and latrines behind the firing line. Twice affronted, and already smouldering with the accumulated resentment of four centuries, Islam arose. At first in Samarkand, later throughout the region, Muslims fell upon Russian army posts and civilian homes. They were ruthlessly put down and by the end of 1916 the revolt had been suppressed, with heavy casualties on both sides. Well over 3,000 Russian civilians were lost in Turkestan alone, which did not include the vastness of the Kazakh Stepnoy Kray, where some of the worst excesses occurred. No one ever counted the Muslim dead, but one unofficial estimate put it at over a million. After the Revolution there was the brief hope of a new beginning, when Lenin and Stalin jointly appealed for the support of Muslims ("all you whose mosques and places of worship have been destroyed, whose customs have been trampled under foot by the tsars and the oppressors of Russia! Your beliefs, your customs, your national and cultural constitutions are from now on free and safe . . . "). But when Muslims sought autonomy from their new masters 5,000 were massacred by the Reds at Khokand early in 1918. This led to the Basmatchi guerrilla movement, which attracted the attention of the disgraced Turkish general Enver Pasha, who declared himself Commander of the Faithful in Central Asia, self-styled Emir of Turkestan, and led the insurgents with some success until he was killed in a skirmish when trying to cross the Amu Dar'ya into Afghanistan in 1922.

As commissar for nationalities, Stalin had offered blandishments in the appeal he made with Lenin in 1917. As Vozhd, the Supreme Leader, he alone was responsible for the collectivisation programme, which was a catastrophe to the Muslims in Central Asia, whose life revolved around land and livestock to the exclusion of everything but their religion. When the communist officials and the Red Army detachments descended on the settlements they were met with resistance, and Russian communities were counter-attacked. Some Uzbeks followed the example of Kirghiz and Kazakhs in conducting a scorched earth policy, which included slaughtering their own beasts rather than submit. Large numbers simply went elsewhere, with all that they could move, among them the entire population of an aul close to the eastern borders, which dismantled its yurts one night and retreated deep into China, taking with it 15,000 cattle and 30,000 sheep. Those who remained found that not only were their possessions at risk under the new order. In 1925 Stalin had been instrumental in launching a Movement of the Godless to rid the land of superstition. Within a few years its functionaries had been given control of all mosques and Islamic seminaries, which were turned into cinemas, night-clubs, dance halls. Funds that the faithful raised to maintain their clergy were declared illegal, the Hadj to Mecca was banned, religious texts, not excluding the Koran itself, were burned. Nothing more outrageous could possibly have been done by Moscow and, when outrage was expressed, the purges, the trials, the deportations, the executions followed. A halt was called only when the Nazis invaded Russia, but by then the damage was irreparable. One and a half million Muslims were conscripted into the Red Army, and of these 800,000 deserted to the Germans as opportunity arose.

There was a very large background to Barak's hostility in Tashkent.

Officially, of course, no such thing as friction between Uzbeks and Slavs existed; and many Uzbeks had always found that it paid to come to terms with the forces of communism, ever since the Revolution. Some, like Sharaf Rashidov and Yadegar Nassreddinova, had done extremely well out of party membership. The Soviet Union could never have survived till now without the complaisance of many indigenous people in the so-called ethnic republics. The official view was most stylishly expressed in Tashkent's State Art Museum, where Vladik and I went one day to browse among Uzbek things that had been collected under the Romanovs. There was a room full of wooden doors and shutters, which had perhaps been rescued from buildings that General Kauffmann destroyed, or maybe from mud-walled dwellings that had simply subsided in the course of time into the desert dust. I had seen shutters like these in many Islamic lands, where the sun was excluded from a home as much as possible, though I had seen none that were more finely wrought. The panels, cracked and splintered in places, but now most carefully preserved, were intricately and wonderfully carved in patterns that strangely resembled Pictish knotwork and that Celtic interlacing which is a glory of the Book of Kells. There was also a set of nineteenth-century chessmen from Bukhara in which the pawns were sheep, the castles were minarets, the bishops were mullahs mounted on donkeys, the knights were princelings on camels, the King was an emir and the Queen looked suspiciously like a belly-dancer.

The top floor of the building housed its paintings, a large

122

proportion from the Soviet era, heroically Realistic with titles like 'The Making of a Bolshevik' or 'You Are Not Alone.' The biggest of them, a huge canvas hung strategically at the top of the staircase to announce the collection – filling the entire wall there, in a strange echo of Fra Angelico's 'Annunciation' at the Convent of S. Marco in Florence – struck the note that was followed inside with very few exceptions. It depicted 'The Proclamation of the Uzbek SSR' and it had been painted by P. P. Benkov in 1940. That was sixteen years after the proclamation, which had been made on the eve of collectivisation in Central Asia. It was not a happy time, though no one would have guessed this from Benkov's work. The setting was some indistinct interior, with very dark drapes overhead that were probably meant to represent the past, from which Light was emerging. A long table cut across the centre of the composition and, behind this, grouped around a bust of Lenin, were Uzbek revolutionaries of both sexes, the women gloriously liberated from the veil. Facing them was a man in kaftan and turban, half-turned towards a crowd which was also costumed in the traditional way, as yet unemancipated into European dress. I think he was saying, "We're with you comrades; aren't we, mates?" There were green lightshades on the table lamps but otherwise the painting was awash with red – in the carpet, on the tablecloth, and in the many flags that were brandished here and there. There wasn't a pensive face in sight; simply a concourse of happy, smiling folk who were clapping enthusiastically, waving flags, holding out the hand of friendship, endorsing the group round Lenin's bust. An alternative title might have been 'Rejoice! Rejoice!' for there was nothing more to it than that. Nor was there a single Russian to disturb the harmony of the piece.

At the Opera House later on, the audience was wholly Slav so far as I could see, and not one of the singers had an Uzbek name. We had gone to a performance of *Iolanta*, one of the less popular things Tchaikovsky composed, for a one-act romance about a princess whose blindness is cured

123

by love. The Opera House had been built just after the war in the theatrical style that Peter the Great brought to Russia from western Europe in the eighteenth century, with gilded mirrors in the marbled foyer, flambeaux mounting the stairs, and golden putti decorating the plush-topped balconies. If it was damaged in the 1966 earthquake it had been restored very well; and, unlike opera in the West, its productions were accessible to everyone. A seat in the second row of the stalls cost 1 rouble 50 kopeks that night. A few hours earlier in the old market I had seen large tomatoes selling for 2.50 roubles apiece. Yet the auditorium reverberated almost emptily, with row after row of unoccupied seats separating one small clump of enthusiasts from the next: army officers and their wives, middle-aged folk in cardigans, a few younger people who looked as if they might be the sons and daughters of the bureaucracy. I doubt whether the place was even one-quarter full.

"But opera is not popular among Russians today," said Vladik. At the age of twenty-eight he had been to the Bolshoi only once, though he had lived in Moscow most of his life.

I was embarrassed when the curtain rose and the singers could see what they were facing for the next couple of hours. The evening reeked of provincial disappointment, for the performance was inadequate, too. The principals were passable but the chorus work was ragged and there was, in effect, no production, no décor above the aspirations of a very local Christmas pantomime. At the end, the cast bowed and curtsied half-heartedly, which was no more than the thin spatter of clapping deserved. That had died before the curtain went down a second time, and the orchestra was already packed up and leaving the pit. I remembered the wild applause that hailed each dancer in the Kazakh beauty contest and felt sad for opera in Uzbekistan.

All Tashkent's verve seemed to be concentrated each night in the dining-room of our hotel, which was huge, with a space for dancing at one end, just beneath a dais with the usual band of musicians and their electronic gear. There

124

was something much more attractive about them than their counterparts in the West. Like the other guitarists and organists I had heard in Central Asia, they eschewed the pelvic thrusts and other posturings, the grotesque haircuts and bizarre accoutrements, that generally divert our audiences from the dismal truth that the sounds they hear aren't up to much. These Soviet instrumentalists – and they invariably represented the local mixture of race – clad in nothing more eye-catching than jeans, tee-shirts, tank tops or leather jackets, stood almost motionless and played their music with a quiet intensity that gave it the appeal of genuine pop art. There was nothing spurious about the vocalist either. He wasn't inciting his audience to lust after him, or to scream hysterically at his glottal range; he was simply doing his best to sing in perfect harmony with the rest of the band.

Yabloki na snegu, rozovyie na belom
Shto zhe nam s nimi delat'
S yablokami na snegu!
Yabloki na snegu v rozovo-nezhnoi kozhe . . .

There was a general rush to the floor when the lads struck up 'Apples,' and this, again, was one place where Slavs and Uzbeks mingled easily on equal terms, shuffling and shaking together to the pulse of the tune. Most nights the place was noisily full, and one evening it was so crowded that Vladik and I had to share a table with a couple of elderly Uzbek men in shapeless and crumpled business suits. They were already beginning to founder over the remnants of their meal, and an almost empty vodka bottle between them told the reason why. Before we managed to order our food, they had obtained a fresh bottle and two more glasses, which were shoved across the table with a nod. I do not remember this as an especially conversational evening, though as time passed it became increasingly convivial, with many a warm toast and expression of goodwill. There was much scribbling of names and addresses on cigarette packets before the

125

end, which was accompanied by an invitation. Our new acquaintances were teachers from the Institute of Literature, and they wanted us to join them for a meal with some colleagues the following day.

That is how we came to be trudging along a very muddy path in suburban Tashkent, as sleet lashed down from a gloomy sky. We had picked up our hosts at the institute and then taken a long ride in a packed tram, which put us down where several hundred yards separated one gigantic housing block from the next, with the wind howling between them as if it were rushing down a mountain pass. As a concession to me, we had recruited a young colleague of our hosts, neither of whom had a word of English. Timur spoke it quite well, with much enthusiasm. We hadn't been on the tram for more than a minute, strap-hanging with two or three strangers wedged between us, before he shouted cheerfully above the racket of the bogies, "Geoffrey, I can't tell you how *thrilled* I am to be sharing this car with you!" Not wishing to be the object of more intimacies at the top of his voice, I nodded amiably and turned away, avoiding the inquisitive eyes of almost all our fellow passengers.

Our destination was a dilapidated wooden cottage at the end of the muddy path. It had a garden at the back in which a sheep and several turkeys looked miserable as they stood in slush beneath the bare branches of apple, apricot and walnut trees. There was also, behind a ramshackle wooden palisade, a privy consisting of a hole in the earth, with two wooden boards on each side, flush with the ground. On entering the cottage I found that we were in a sort of farmhouse kitchen, a large room in which both the eating and the cooking took place. It was also a depository of many parts. Old chests of drawers were piled high with yellowing academic journals. Leaning against cupboards or littering the floor were a variety of objects, from skis and garden implements, to flat-irons and a small transformer. Presiding over this bric-à-brac was a large sepia photograph, high on a wall, of a grey-bearded man in uniform who looked as if he might have been something quite important in the Imperial

Russian Navy. Yet, apart from Vladik and myself, everyone in the room was a native of Uzbekistan.

Already there when we arrived were two young women from the institute who had been dragooned into cooking the meal. The men draped themselves around the table at once and began to chew nuts and dried fruit, which had been laid out to await our coming, while the women busied themselves amid steaming pots on a gas stove. Cornered by Timur, I was cross-examined about my knowledge of Uzbek literature, which was non-existent, unless I was allowed to admit an awareness of Avicenna – who was born near Bukhara a thousand years ago – on the grounds that he composed some verse, although most of his writings were philosophical and scientific rather than literary. Indeed, the only contemporary writer from Central Asia I had read was the Kirghiz novelist Chingiz Aitmatov. I told Timur that I seriously doubted whether there were a hundred people in Britain who could even drop the names of two living Uzbek writers into a literary conversation, much less claim an acquaintance with their work. His eyebrows rose almost to the crown of his prematurely bald head, and his voice squeaked with astonishment.

"You mean that you do not know of our best-sellers?"

"I'm afraid not. But then, I don't suppose many Uzbeks have read George Mackay Brown or R. S. Thomas."

"Please?"

"The first is an Orcadian, the second a Welshman. They're both very fine writers, and best-sellers in their parts of the country."

"An Orcadian, I think, is someone who lives in Arcady? Yes?"

I thought of the snug and winding lanes of Stromness, Alan Stewart making prehistory live again in the dunes at Skara Brae, seabirds wheeling round the cliffs on Hoy. Arcady it was, compared with this dull and polluted city.

All our conversation limped along like this, and the two professors did nothing to enliven it, being more interested in gossiping between themselves, with occasional cries of

127

encouragement to the two women skivvying at the stove. When they had finished cooking and served the food, they hovered uncertainly until one of the old men indicated that they should sit, too. They perched at the end of the table, so that there was significant space between them and the men. Their grandmothers would have been in purdah, obliged to prepare our meal out of sight, certainly kept well out of the way as long as strangers were in the house. So this propinquity represented a considerable advance and was entirely due to communism, I did not doubt. But there were limits, even now. I tried to draw the women into our talk, and they flashed smiles of pleasure across the kitchen when they realised I was directing questions at them. Timur's Uzbek translations of my English were perfunctory, discouraging more than monosyllabic reply. So I tried my lame Russian, at which he and one of the professors barged in with their own versions, which produced the same effect. The women lapsed into shy silence again, while men held the floor inadequately. Even after acculturation at this sophisticated level, some of Islam's dogmas were relatively undisturbed.

We went in search of the deepest dogmas next day, and for once we had Barak accompanying us. He had arranged for me to meet the Rector of the Tashkent Imam Al Bukhari Institute, which was the highest Islamic seminary in the USSR. It lay within the only part of the old city that had been spared destruction in the earthquake. There were narrow streets with windowless walls of baked mud. Windows would have overlooked a domestic yard in every dwelling, Islamic privacy in its most highly traditional form. Beyond the claustrophobia of these alleyways, the institute was housed in a series of low buildings on the edge of a spacious square, with a stunted form of minaret rising from one corner. Barak left Vladik and me on a verandah and vanished through a door at the far end, while we kicked our heels. The sound of recitation came from a room close by, where half a dozen youths sat at desks, learning the Koran by rote. Presently a boy came to lead us to the head of the institute, and we were ushered into a room where Barak, too, awaited us. When we were invited to sit round a table he arranged himself next to the cleric, opposite us. It was a pointed gesture. There was no question whose side he was on.

I had expected some senior in such a post, but the man who greeted us seemed so preposterously young that for a moment I wondered whether he was a subordinate, sitting in for the rector. He bore an uncanny resemblance to a Benedictine abbot I had once known, who had been elected superior of his monastery at the age of thirty-seven, when he still looked a decade younger. Had this man been clad in a black cassock instead of a white one, had he not worn the white skullcap of Muslim orthodoxy on his head, had his complexion run to rosy rather than sallow cheeks, there would have been no telling the two religious apart. His manner was quiet and his smile attractive, but it soon became clear that he was extremely guarded in everything he said. He told me little things, some of which I already knew: that the institute had opened in 1971 and contained fifty students, including a number from South Yemen, Vietnam, Bulgaria and Afghanistan; that Islam throughout the Soviet Union was of the Sunni rite except in Azerbaijan, whose Muslims were Shias like their neighbours across the border in Iran; that there were eighteen mosques functioning in Tashkent now and that this very month had seen five more reopened throughout Uzbekistan, after long sequestration by the state; that relations with the state had steadily improved since new regulations had been promulgated in 1971. I also discovered that pilgrimage to Mecca was now allowed again, for some at least. His visiting card said that he was Al-Haj Zahid Abdulkadir.

His caution became evident when I tried to draw him on to contentious ground. I asked him if there had been any trouble in Uzbekistan comparable to the riots which had occurred twice in Alma-Ata in the past few years, in which people had been killed.* The rector said these were local

* In 1986, thirty were killed in a riot which sprang from plain Kazakh hostility towards Russians. In 1980 four had died at a demonstration over the burial of a Muslim officer killed during the war in Afghanistan.

129

matters elsewhere, and he had no knowledge of them. When I put the question in a different way, Barak answered for him.

"We have no riots here – yet."

I ignored him and tried another one. It must, I said, have been a difficult time for Muslims in Uzbekistan when some of their men were fighting other Muslims in Afghanistan. Yes, said the rector, it had been a difficult time.

Silence, and a faint smile on Barak's face.

I made another attempt. It had struck me that not once on this journey had I heard the muezzin's call to prayer, though his amplified voice usually carries to every corner of every Muslim community I have known. I had questioned Timur about this and his answer had been comical: "You see, now there is no need for the call, because people now have watches in these times." The rector considered my question for a moment, testing it for possible hazards. Then he replied that if I cared to stay until later in the day I would hear the muezzin call from the minaret of the institute, though it would be in his natural voice, without electrical assistance.

One other thing I was curious to know of this mild-mannered hierarch. Just before I left England there had been a demonstration by Muslims in Bradford against Salman Rushdie's book *The Satanic Verses*, and only two days before I reached Tashkent, as I discovered by listening to a BBC news bulletin, the Ayatollah Khomeini had issued his fatwa calling upon Muslims throughout the world to ensure that Rushdie was killed. I had not read the book, but I didn't doubt that it was deeply offensive to them. Everything of Rushdie's that I had read was deeply offensive to someone; offensiveness, together with a high talent for fantasy, was his most notable stock-in-trade. And if that was in his mind he had not only a right but a duty to utter it. The idea that a medieval madman in Teheran should have put the black spot on any writer for fulfilling his principal obligation to society was insufferable.

Here, in the depths of Central Asia, the rector was well

130

aware of the scandal Rushdie's book had caused. Two days earlier, he said, there had been demands "from all over Uzbekistan" for the burning of the book, and for a protest to be lodged at the British Embassy in Moscow. He himself did not believe the death penalty should be carried out, but he thought the author should be punished for blasphemy under British law. I got the impression that an independent party line was still being worked out by the Muslims of the Soviet Union, and that the principal of their chief seminary was uncomfortable in offering me an opinion of something that was no more than hearsay to him.

Barak, on the other hand, was gloating. "I think he doesn't have too much longer to live," he said, and sniggered unpleasantly.

Al-Haj Zahid Abdulkadir belonged,I suspect, to an Islamic tradition I had always been able to respect, for virtues that can be discovered in any faith or none at all. I had warmed to such Muslims in many lands, and I had often added my own inchoate entreaties to their rigorous prayer when they submitted themselves at the devotional hour. I had done this in the company of nomads in the middle of the North African desert, with students and artisans at the great Badshahi Mosque in Lahore, even in the makeshift place of worship that servants of the Great Eastern Hotel in Calcutta had contrived in its boiler room. With them all I had felt a community of reverence, of gentleness, of tolerance for another's way of trying to understand mysterious things. But there was an alternative face of Islam, just as there was an unattractive side to every religion. It was narrow and it believed in intimidation; in making demands which ought to be requests, in shameless bullying and in terrorism. Of this Islam I was heartily sick.

131

6

Bukhara

Bukhara was of the desert and could have been nowhere else. Reaching Timbuktu after weeks of riding camels across the Sahara had once been a bit like this. Coming to Jaisalmer, castellated on its hill amid the sands of Rajasthan, was much the same. But I could think of no other places I knew which quite conveyed these contradictory sensations of sanctuary and menace, remote from all assistance, at one and the same time. This was in spite of the fact that the outskirts of Bukhara were as commonplace as any suburb of Tashkent, though the proletarian blocks were much less extensive and far smaller, and the roads were not nearly so wide. What mattered was that they led to an ancient centre which still spoke powerfully of the caravan and the bazaar, the piety of the ages and the cruelty of unhindered power.

Bukhara's heyday had been during the time of the Persian Samanids, who made it their capital in the ninth century over a territory that included the whole of modern Uzbekistan and Tadzhikistan, with much of Iran and Afghanistan besides. Within a hundred years it had a population of 300,000 and contained 250 madrassas, which schooled pupils from places as far away as Yemen and Andalusia: but it was not only a centre of religious instruction. Its royal library is said to have contained 45,000 books, which raised Bukhara to the level of Baghdad, and one of the beneficiaries was the polymathic Husain ibn Abdullah ibn Sina, more widely known as Avicenna. Not only polymath but prodigy, for at the age of eighteen he cured the ruler of a chronic illness and was rewarded with access to the library, to which he presently added many texts of his own, as philosopher, astronomer, mathematician and poet as well as doctor of medicine. He was also a linguist who translated Aristotle into Arabic, and a gifted musician who was simultaneously so active in the politics of the court that for several years he was its Grand Vizier. But his major work was the *Qanun*, his Canon of Medicine, an encyclopaedia of medical knowledge in China, India, Persia, Egypt and Greece from sources that spanned ten centuries. This was a compendium of such unique consequence that a Pope eventually issued a bull authorising its study in the medical faculties of Europe, and it maintained its position as a basis of universal teaching until the great scientific discoveries of the nineteenth century at last outdated it.

As Vladik and I drove in from the surrounding wastes the first trace of that age we encountered was a length of the old city wall which some Soviet bulldozer had lately cleft asunder so that a new road could be put through. On either side of the fresh tarmacadam and kerbstones (illuminated at night by tall sodium lamps) the crumbling ramparts of ancient Bukhara stretched away across ground that had been churned to mud by earth-moving equipment. A clutter of telegraph poles and electricity pylons overlooked the tumbledown bastions which extended from the wall at

133

intervals, and my heart sank at the miserable sight of history not only neglected but violated by my contemporaries. This was a premature depression. Just up the road the tarmac swerved round an open expanse of ground which formed a kind of cordon sanitaire between the old city and the new. To cross it was to disappear at once into a labyrinth that was still, as it had always been, turned in upon itself protectively from the desert. Here was the ancient and still recognisable oasis.

The blank walls of houses, such as we had seen in the surviving fragment of Tashkent's old quarter, formed the sides of every alley here. They were made of hard-baked mud mixed with straw, a material that sounds less durable than it is, well able to withstand any climate that does not include heavy rain, which is practically unknown in Central Asia. These walls were broken only by doors whose most perfect examples I had admired in the Tashkent museum; doors enclosing entrances so small that everyone but a child would have to bend low in order to pass through. They were not as finely carved as the ones in the museum and most of them had been painted a deep blue or green. Not one stood ajar, so it was impossible to peep into the courtyard beyond. The effect was not only one of privacy guarded obsessively, but of claustrophobia, too. For the alleys were narrow and the flat roofs high enough for nothing else to be visible but the sky directly above. And because these alleys twisted and dog-legged erratically, it was very easy to lose all sense of direction and return to a starting point without the slightest inkling that one had gone astray. It was like trying to find a way to the middle of some gigantic maze made of baked mud.

The middle had a glory I had never come across before. By this I do not mean that it was more glorious than Fatehpur Sikri or Agra, or the old quarters of Lahore or Istanbul or Cairo, or anywhere else that had captivated me with its treasury of classical Islamic architecture; simply that nothing else I had seen was as marvellous in this particular way. There was the splendour of domes clad in turquoise tiles,

134

which glowed with a celestial light. On some a number of the tiles had fallen off, so that the fabric beneath was exposed to give the dome a mouldering appearance. On others the weathering of the years had been repaired, and the dome rose in perfect plumpness above its mosque or its madrassa. Each was nippled with a finial which, on the unrestored domes, had invariably sprouted a strange growth of vegetation, a pile of sticks and grasses which looked too top-heavy to stay put. These were the nests of storks, for which Bukhara used to be famous. But a nearby swamp, caused by that same water supply which created the oasis, had been drained a few years ago, thus depriving the birds of their feeding ground, and they had not been seen since.

There was the splendour of the high portals to each of the religious buildings which, seen from afar, appeared to be as insubstantial as pieces of scenery in a film studio, with height and width but almost no depth. This illusion occurred because the portals invariably allowed access to a spacious courtyard and rose far above the level of the surrounding walls. They had more depth than was at first apparent, almost an interior shaped like the apse of a Christian church, and this was sometimes honeycombed with that form of Islamic roof-vaulting known as muqarnas. The same turquoise that glazed the domes was repeated in the intricate patterns decorating the frontage of these portals, where they mingled with tiles of ultramarine, russet, primrose, amber and viridian in dazzling abstractions, writhed in herbaceous tendrils around archways, and were empanelled as urns full of cornflowers the size of chrysanthemums. As with the domes, some of the portals had fallen into disrepair with the disfiguring loss of many coloured fragments, but in almost every case enough of the original composition remained to convey the sensational lustre that had once been there.

Above all, there was the splendour of structures which revealed the full imaginative possibilities of building in brick. This was not the harshly pink and smooth brick of my childhood, made to withstand the corrosive fumes of the

135

Lancashire cotton industry and in time becoming blackened with its soot; nor was it the rougher and mellower red brick that had beautified places as far apart as Massachusetts, Shropshire and Tuscany. The brick of Bukhara came with the texture and colour of its desert sand. And even when the medieval bricklayers of the city were bent on utility more than decoration, they produced buildings with a sculptural quality that in form and proportion was memorable. Such were the bazaars that attracted the caravan trade, each specialising in a particular commodity: Taq i Zargaran, where the goldsmiths worked, Taq i Talpakfuroshon, where skullcaps and other garments could be obtained, Taq i Sarrafon, where the moneylenders crouched. There were others, each housed beneath its own circle of brick cupolas, all entered through a high brick portal with an ogee arch. From the outside the pattern of these shallow domes suggested some intimate rite within. Inside, mighty pillars of brick curved into low vaultings, with large doorways into the different shops, and the general effect was curiously as if a Saracen had collaborated with a Norman in the design of a cathedral crypt. What they needed was the bustle of commerce on the medieval scale, but what little trade I saw was confined to the shops and was there conducted with almost European restraint.

There was much fanciful decoration in the khaki bricks of Bukhara, so that until you had walked to within a few paces of some gateway you would have sworn that the patterns on either side of the entrance had been graven in stone. The most gorgeously decorated building of all stood in a little park, and in summer it would have been virtually hidden amidst trees in full foliage, for it did not rise higher than the topmost branch. This was the tenth-century mausoleum of the Samanids, essentially a dome mounted on a cube, and everything in its construction was made from brick. The dome was twice encircled by projecting brick studs, and there was a brick lantern at the very apex of the roof. The cube's topmost corners were each embellished with a beehive shape and the dome sat within these, perfectly austere had it not been for the lantern and the studs. The cube was another matter, so completely ornate that it was almost too much; and would have been if the patterns had not been so marvellously controlled. Just below the top courses was a gallery of arches, ten on each side of the cube. Below that the full power of someone's imagination had been unloosed. There were portals on each side of the building; there were apparently free-standing columns at each of its corners and all of these, together with the intervening walls, were spectacular with incident as the courses were laid in counterpoint, then differently again, and as they came in many contrasting shapes. Someone obsessed with the possibilities inherent in brick had been trying to push variety to its limits; and it had worked superbly because everything had been in harmony, without irregularity. As I walked round the mausoleum and studied it from different angles and varying range, it sometimes seemed to have the texture of elaborate basketwork, while at others it was almost like filigree, a lattice through which an evening breeze might cool the summer heat inside. I could well believe that its reputation was deserved: this might not only be the finest decorative brickwork in Islam, but in the whole world, sacred and profane.

It had one tremendous competitor in Bukhara, in the Kalan Tower, which rose 150 feet or so into the air above the centre of the city and was said to be the tallest building in Central Asia. As the eye travelled from a sturdy base up the tapering courses of brickwork to a gallery and then the parapet on top, it traversed a score or more of different designs, encircling the column one after another in thick bands of such tactile appeal that I wished this object – which had been built in the twelfth century as a minaret but looked like a lighthouse – could be reduced to the scale of a toy so that I might enjoy the sensation of stroking it. When it was a hundred years old, Genghiz Khan laid siege to Bukhara, which he took on the third day after the usual butchery, though on this occasion he allowed those Bukhariots who survived and surrendered to leave with only the clothes they

137

were wearing. As he rode into the city he reined in his horse before the tower and sat looking at it for minutes, holding a finger to his mouth in a curious token of amazement. Then he ordered that every building in Bukhara should be destroyed, with the exception of this one. The Samanid mausoleum also escaped the destruction, but only because the Mongols did not know it was there. It had been buried in some mighty sandstorm ages before they arrived and, because the dynasty it commemorated had been superseded by a different line of rulers, nobody had been interested in digging it out.

Once before on this journey I had examined a column like this, when Evgeni and I had been driving close to the Tien Shan range in Kirghizia and came to the remains of the Burana Tower, which was a little older, not quite as richly decorated, and partially demolished as a result of a nineteenth-century earthquake. I had measured the bricks there and found that they coincided exactly with the wafer-thin bricks that went into the building of Mohenjodaro, the Bronze Age ruins in the lower valley of the River Indus, a thousand miles to the south of the Tien Shan. This may have been fortuitous, but it could equally have had some small anthropological significance. One of the great population theories has always held that a cradle of mankind was somewhere on the great steppe, from which there were simultaneous migrations west towards Europe and south into the Indian subcontinent. The bricks in Kirghizia were not nearly as old as those of the Indus Valley, but there was no reason why they might not have belonged to the same tradition.

In spite of the fact that the Burana Tower was freestanding on the very edge of the steppe beside the mountain wall, it was known to have been built as a religious edifice, for although all traces of any attendant mosque had disappeared from the site there was a Muslim graveyard close by. Yet it would almost surely have had another purpose, as would the Kalan Tower on the edge of the desert in Bukhara. A peculiarity of Central Asia and the adjacent lands to the south and the west is the frequency with which such towers appear in the middle of nowhere. One of the most famous is the Gunbad i Qabus, the great brick decagon which rises to a conical peak not far from the shores of the Caspian in Iran. It was built to accommodate the remains of an eleventh-century king, suspended in a glass coffin high above the ground. Even more eerily alone in the desert of south-east Iran is a nameless tower, truncated like the one I'd seen in Kirghizia and with a certain amount of brick-nogging comparable to the decoration in Bukhara, whose purpose must have been that of beacon for the guidance of caravans travelling great distances across an otherwise featureless waste. Scholars have long been confident that even where towers were built as part of some religious complex, in which they had a liturgical significance – as a minaret from which the muezzin would summon the faithful to prayer – they had an alternative role as a marker for the traveller from afar; possibly as a watchtower for the community as well, from which early warning might be given of impending attack. Certainly the resemblance between the Kalan Tower and a lighthouse was too striking to be ignored. They would have burned pitch on that parapet above the gallery, to steer to safety some important caravan whose arrival was anticipated on an extremely black and moonless night.

The Kalan Tower had another function besides the religious and the navigational, and this one typified the deep streak of cruelty that runs like a fault line through Bukhara's past. When the Tsar's envoy Nicholas Ignatieff reached Bukhara in 1858, intent on making a trade treaty with the emir, he observed that the path to the ruler's dwelling "was flanked by blackened heads on pikes, trophies of justice and revenge." The emir's predecessor had ordered the bludgeoning to death of an Italian watchmaker, Giovanni Orlandi of Parma, though no one seemed quite sure whether it was because he refused to become a Muslim or because he allowed the emir's clock to stop. Another of these potentates, aware that he had not much longer to live, summoned

139

his favourite wife and three daughters and had them killed beside his bed so that he could be quite sure no one else would enjoy them after he'd gone. For every ruler, the Kalan Tower was a regular instrument of execution. Criminals, or the merely dissident, were taken struggling up its winding stairs and allowed to see the city spread far below. Then they were tied in a sack and thrown off the parapet. According to Gustav Krist, who visited the city both during and after the Great War, this continued well into the twentieth century. When the last of the Tsars, Nicholas II, let it be known that he thought little of this practice in what was by then effectively a client emirate, the ruler briefly decapitated his subjects instead; but with the Russians otherwise preoccupied in the war, death by jaculation was resumed.

This was not the only horror discovered by the Red Army when it took possession of Bukhara in 1920. Elsewhere in the emirate, on the caravan route to Ferghana, the soldiers investigated a serai which was the subject of rumours circulating in the city's bazaars. They found in its capacious cellars a very large and very savage brown bear, together with the bones of several hundred human beings, which covered the floor in a layer two or three feet deep. Here was the solution to a long-standing mystery: the disappearance of caravans travelling that way, together with their valuable cargoes of gold, turquoise, carpets, silk, tobacco, corn, wool and weapons. They had been vanishing without trace for many years, and the full gruesome story finally emerged at a Revolutionary Tribunal established by the new Soviet authority in Bukhara.

A bandit named Khoja Khan was responsible for seizing the camels and their loads, while his nephew was entertaining the drovers and travelling merchants in the caravanserai, of which he was bashi. He plied them with liquor, most notably with tarantula brandy, a concoction that had always been known and used in Turkestan, in spite of the fact that to Muslims all strong drink is harram. It was made after catching a number of poisonous spiders and putting them

140

into a jar with pieces of dried apple and apricot, which they bit and injected with their venom. The fruit was then removed and mixed with grapes, for distillation. Quite a small glassful of the resulting liquid would swiftly produce paralysis. And when the victims of the caravanserai bashi became helpless, he pitched them into his cellar to feed his bear, which he had carefully trained to relish human flesh. At his trial he boasted that he had disposed of 411 men in this way. He was condemned to death by the Russians but they never executed him. Some local people broke into his prison cell and hauled him off into the night. They tethered him, on the end of a long rope, to a couple of camels. Then they stuffed peppers into the anuses of these unfortunate beasts, which galloped away furiously into the desert, dragging the mass murderer behind them. His skeleton was found out there a few days later, its bits and pieces of bone scattered over a wide area.

The rulers of Bukhara held court in the Arg, whose general design was much like that of the citadel I had seen in Peshawar several years before, though that one had been equipped with traffic lights, to regulate the comings and goings of the Khyber Rifles and other troops of the Pakistan Army. The Arg was without such modern trappings and there was still much ancient menace residing in those sandy battlements (brick, again) which sloped high and inward above the surrounding ground. Within living memory it would have taken some courage to go up the ramp and between the two towers of the gatehouse, knowing what had awaited far too many predecessors on the inside. The ornate clock which the wretched Orlandi had made for the Emir Nasrullah in return for his life, and which may have been the death of him in the end, used to hang incongruously above the entrance arch; but, I was told, someone had taken it down at the time of the Revolution 'for cleaning' and it has not been since. The citadel had been turned into a museum by the Soviet authorities, who did not attempt to minimise the horrors from which Bukhariots had been saved by the forces of communism. There was a photograph of

141

the last Emir of Bukhara, a portly little despot with a black beard, who took himself off to exile among kinsmen in Afghanistan at the Bolshevik approach. Only a short time before, his vassal princes had been obliged to approach his throne in the Arg by crawling on all fours; and they did not nearly have the worst of things. His saurian gaze now fell on some photographs hanging on the wall opposite his picture, showing the effect of seventy-five lashes on a man's back, administered for some trifling offence. Elsewhere in the room was a graphic painting of some poor loser about to have his throat cut judicially; and another of a thief whose hand was being amputated.

But no emir was quite as vicious as Nasrullah, whose long rule began in 1826, after he had murdered his father and his elder brother; and then, to guard against any possibility of fratricide, his three younger brothers as well. Behind the Arg was the Zindan, the prison in which the emirs of Bukhara held their captives. Every Friday the common criminals were allowed out of the Zindan in their shackles to beg for food among the people thronging the marketplace below; and on what the good Muslims of the city were disposed to donate on Islam's holiest day of the week, these prisoners lived until the following Friday. Some survived this form of victualling and others did not. One group of prisoners was not even permitted this indulgence; and for them Nasrullah devised a captivity that was truly the inspiration of an evil mind. He consigned them to the Sia Chat, the Black Well, which was a chamber excavated underground with no light and no access except through a small rectangle some twenty feet above the floor. The chamber had been walled with bricks, as if to emphasise the hopelessness of attempted escape, and the only way out was through the small hole above, as long as someone dropped down at least a rope. Christian kings had also built dungeons as awful as this, but the Emir Nasrullah's imagination went beyond entombment. His prisoners shared the Sia Chat with rats, scorpions, lice, cockroaches and other vermin specially introduced for the purpose of

142

torment, including sheep ticks which burrowed into flesh and made dreadful sores.

The museum curators had dramatised the Black Well by placing a couple of dummies in it, and tourists had responded by chucking coins into the pit, while the dummies looked in supplication at the little rectangle of light, one squatting in the middle of the floor, the other leaning exhausted against the wall. They were shackled, they were bearded, they wore the local headcloth and other desert clothes, but they were unmistakably European. They were Stoddart and Conolly, and I had waited a long time to see where they met their end.

The first of them to fall into Nasrullah's clutches was Charles Stoddart, a truculent half-colonel in the British Army, who had been sent to persuade the Emir that his interests would be best served by an alliance with Queen Victoria rather than with Tsar Nicholas I. He had made the early mistake of ignoring all the niceties of oriental protocol, deeply insulting his host; and his offence was compounded by his not having brought any message in Her Majesty's own hand. Nasrullah did not care to be addressed as an equal by the Governor-General of India, whose signature was attached to the document Stoddart conveyed. Three days after his arrival, the Englishman was flung into the Black Well, where he stayed for six months, while his captors vowed that he would be put to death unless he converted to Islam. Not until he was taken out of the pit to watch his grave being dug, and was told that he would be buried alive in it, did his nerve go. He allowed himself to be circumcised and he recited the Kulna, the Muslim profession of faith. The Emir thereupon gave him some clean clothes and installed him in quarters above ground, where he enjoyed a measure of freedom to do almost anything but leave Bukhara. In time, he was even allowed to move into a house occupied by a Russian mission, which arrived in the city almost three years after him with instructions similar to his own, to win the confidence of the Emir. Colonel Butenyov and Lieutenant-Colonel Stoddart, European soldier-emissaries thrown together in the wilds of Central Asia, seem to have got on remarkably well, in spite of their professional rivalry.

Meanwhile, Captain Arthur Conolly, of the Bengal Light Cavalry, had set out from India with instructions to form alliances with the khans of Khokand and Khiva and then, if it were at all possible, to retrieve Stoddart from what seemed no more than a highly embarrassing position to the British authorities in London and Calcutta. It is likely that the rescue operation fired Conolly's imagination at least as much as the diplomacy, for he was a romantic adventurer who had just been jilted, and was also a Christian zealot who had heard of his countryman's apostasy. He pressed on towards Bukhara even after the rulers of both Khiva and Khokand warned him that Nasrullah could not be trusted by other Muslims, let alone by anyone else. He reached the city, in fact, just as the Emir and his troops were returning from a victorious sortie into Khokand, where they had butchered the khan and his entire family. Within days, Conolly was put under house arrest with Stoddart, who left his Russian sanctuary in order to be with his fellow officer. A month later both had been cast into the pit, while Colonel Butenyov tried to intercede on their behalf without success. The Russians were preparing to withdraw their mission, more than willing to take the Englishmen to safety with them, but Nasrullah would have none of it. When Butenyov and his men left Bukhara, Stoddart and Conolly were doomed.

They might not have been if the British had properly appreciated that they were dealing with a shrewd as well as a pitiless maniac, whose self-esteem was no less than that of the British monarch, and whose power, unlike hers, was not limited by a parliament. If Nasrullah's vanity had been soothed by a missive from Windsor Castle at any stage of Stoddart's captivity, the Englishman would almost certainly have walked out of Bukhara loaded with presents: but the grandest thing the Emir received was a snub administered by Lord Palmerston. If a brigade of the East India

144

Company's Army, which at this time was campaigning successfully in Afghanistan, had been known to be marching north from Kabul with instructions to bring Stoddart and Conolly back at all costs, Nasrullah would probably have met it with open arms and an ingratiating smile, for he had a tyrant's respect for superior force. Instead, he was able to play cat and mouse with his captives, and this was closely related to the progress of the British military intervention to the south.

The British invaded Afghanistan in 1839, a few months after Stoddart accepted Islam, and as long as they could maintain their puppet Shah Shuja on the throne in Kabul, Stoddart was treated leniently. It was Conolly's misfortune to reach Bukhara not long before the Afghans rose against the British with such ferocity that they caused the invaders to retreat in one of the great disasters of military history. Early in January 1842 some 16,000 British troops and camp followers marched out of Kabul on the road back to the Khyber Pass and India. Ten days later, a solitary survivor reached the British fort at Jalalabad. By then a journal Conolly was keeping (and which miraculously reached his sister in London twenty years later) was clearly anticipating the worst. He had been confined for eighty-three days when he wrote that Nasrullah possessed "the deliberate malice of a demon, questioning and raising our hopes and ascertaining conditions only to see how our hearts were going on in the process of breaking". On June 17th, 1842, the Englishmen were taken, with their hands tied, to the square in front of the Arg, where a great number of Bukhariots had gathered to see what happened next. Stoddart, who had been held in the city for three and a half years by then, had his head cut off first. Conolly was offered clemency if he would accept Islam, but he refused and was also beheaded with a knife.

Arthur Conolly may have been the man who coined the phrase The Great Game, for it came to light first among his papers, when these were being examined by the imperial historian J. W. Kaye. He was certainly romantic enough to have anticipated his Central Asian adventure in such terms, and so were scores of other British officers and civil servants who spent the nineteenth century on intelligence missions in the wild lands to the north of India, parleying with rulers in places like Bukhara, collecting information about tribal loyalties and strengths, spreading rumours when the moment seemed ripe, dangling promises that might or might not be kept. They were in competition with similar agents from Russia, and the object of the exercise in each case was to secure the political ascendancy over the independent territories which formed a buffer between the realm of the Tsar and the empire of the Queen. Not all who participated in the Game were young men. One of the first and most remarkable players was the veterinary surgeon William Moorcroft, who was fifty-eight when he reached Bukhara just before Nasrullah seized the throne. It had taken him six years to struggle there from India, ostensibly in search of new bloodstock to invigorate the East India Company's stud in Bengal. After five months in the oasis he had established a network of spies with a communications system of secret signs, and had reported details of tsarist infiltration at Bukhara, which seemed so improbable to his superiors in Calcutta – the information was, in fact, remarkably accurate – that they decided Moorcroft was a slightly unbalanced Russophobe.

Nor were the players on the British side invariably Europeans. In 1862 Lieutenant T. G. Montgomerie, a mapmaking engineer with the Survey of India, began to train the best of his native staff for clandestine operations in the border regions of Central Asia and Tibet. Already skilled in taking precise measurements of distance, direction and altitude for straightforward cartography, these Indians were now taught how to walk at an identical pace, whether going up or downhill or on the flat, and how to keep count of the paces they took in a day or between chosen points. They were given new identities as pilgrims and other innocents, and they were sent off with their Muslim rosaries and their Buddhist prayer wheels and their staves and begging bowls, all of which were modified for nefarious purposes, to collect

146

information of every kind, including the lie of the land. These were the pundits, an exceptionally brave band of men who would have suffered hideous punishments had they been discovered in their true role as British spies. When Rudyard Kipling wrote *Kim* he modelled Hurry Chunder Mookerjee on one of the best of them, Sarat Chandra Das; and Colonel Creighton, presiding over Kim's unusual education, was almost certainly Montgomerie.

The Great Game between the British and the Russians in Central Asia really originated in the meeting between Napoleon and Alexander I at Tilsit in 1807, when they not only made peace, but plotted a joint operation against British India. Within a few years the French threat had disappeared, but the Russian hazard steadily increased throughout the nineteenth century as the Tsars almost annually pushed their frontiers further south. This, at least, was how things looked to the British, who fought two Afghan wars in that period in the vain hope of controlling an historic buffer zone: and the many garrisons they maintained on the North-West Frontier throughout their time in India betrayed a fear that the tribesmen there might make an alliance with their blood brothers in Afghanistan, and beyond in Turkestan, which would assist a Russian passage over the Hindu Kush. When, in 1880, it was believed that the Tsar's armies were poised to take Herat as a preliminary to invasion, the Duke of Argyll made some resounding puns in Parliament about Merv-ousness. By then the Russians had not only annexed most of Central Asia, but they had begun to build roads and railways across it, so that a journey to Bukhara was no longer as heroic as it had been when Moorcroft, Stoddart and Conolly went there. In spite of political tension between London and St Petersburg, it was possible for a future Viceroy of India to travel quite openly by train to within a dozen miles of the great oasis, which had been a Russian protectorate for twenty years by the time he arrived in 1888.

The Hon. George Nathaniel Curzon MP actually stayed at the Russian Residence, where he created a sensation by unpacking his india rubber bath, without which he never travelled far off the beaten track. He found that although mass-produced Russian goods flooded the bazaars, Singer sewing machines stitched up desert clothes, and kerosene lamps were overtaking candles made of mutton fat, the Emir of Bukhara, not yet thirty years old, still ruled in the ancient way. He maintained a harem of women and a seraglio of dancing boys as well. He not only had criminals thrown from the Kalan Tower, but sanctioned even uglier deaths. Days before Curzon arrived, a murderer had been beaten with sticks and slashed with knives before having his eyelids cut off, after which he was tied to the tail of a donkey and dragged to the marketplace. There he was quartered and thrown to the dogs.

Central Asia was tsarist Russia's India in many respects. It was acquired in much the same fashion, by a combination of stealth and belligerence, and it became a very useful marketplace for Russian industry, later a source of raw materials. But India was never the home of British settlers on anything like the scale of Russian colonisation here, and there were other notable differences between the two imperial possessions. The number of Russian soldiers garrisoning Central Asia was approximately the same as the number of British troops on the subcontinent, though the population of India was thirty times greater. Neither the Russian soldiers nor the officials were ever required to learn any of the languages spoken by the Kazakhs, the Uzbeks, the Kirghiz or the other inhabitants, and few of them ever did; whereas in India every civil servant faced an annual examination in at least one local tongue, and British officers were strongly discouraged from speaking English with their Indian troops. At the height of the Raj, although every educated Indian became in greater or lesser degree anglicised, the native culture flourished as abundantly as ever alongside the alien ways: shop signs and newspapers appeared in English, but never did this affect the use of Arabic, Devanagiri or other Indian scripts in private or in public. Not once in Central Asia, except in the old tiles decorating mosques and religious schools, had I come across a local

148

calligraphy. Every sign was inscribed in the Cyrillic alphabet.

It was natural that the establishment of Bolshevik authority so close to the northern limits of the subcontinent would appeal to those Indians who wanted a revolution against British rule. Many years ago, not long before he died, the Bengali patriot Muzaffar Ahmad told me how he and a number of other dissidents had struggled over the snowbound mountains to reach Termez, on the frontier between Afghanistan and modern Uzbekistan. A military band of the new Red Army then played them aboard a train which took them to Tashkent. Awaiting them there was Lenin's protégé M. N. Roy, another Bengali who had left India in 1915 with ambitions to raise a fighting force that would drive the British from his home.* Lenin had provided him with a couple of trains which travelled under heavily armed guard from Moscow down to Central Asia, carrying not only guns and ammunition, but a quantity of bullion and several dismantled aeroplanes that were to be reassembled at their destination, with a view to air raids on India when the moment was right. In Tashkent, Roy had established an Indian military school, and it was here that Muzaffar Ahmad and his friends were introduced to the mechanics of the machine gun and received their first lessons in political philosophy. It was here, also, that in 1920 the Indian Communist Party was formed. Within twelve months the first party members were slipping back over the mountains with plans to subvert their fellow-countrymen by propaganda and industrial action. Open warfare was no longer an option, and the dismantled biplanes never took off. Lenin had peremptorily closed Roy's Tashkent establishment, at the insistence of Lloyd George and his government. It was the price of an Anglo–Soviet Trade Agreement, which the Russians needed much more than an uprising below the Khyber Pass.

* M. N. Roy was how he styled himself in his revolutionary period.
His real name was Manabendranath Bhattacharya.

149

I had hoped to find traces of all this activity when I was in Tashkent; at least a building that might be remembered for its association with that time. But no one had heard of these matters, not even the intelligentsia in the Institute of Literature. Helpfully, they canvassed their colleagues in the history department of the university, who were no better informed. But, someone recalled, an Indian Prime Minister had once dropped dead at a conference in Tashkent. Was I aware of that? Lal Bahadur Shastri's heart attack appeared to be the only known connection between their city and India. It was all very disappointing.

And here in Bukhara faces were just as blank when I asked about Roy, who had played a small but memorable part in its translation from client emirate to Soviet oblast. As a principal of the Central Asiatic Bureau of the Comintern, he had come to the city with General Frunze and his troops in order to supervise the transfer of civil power. He announced that not only were the four hundred women in the royal harem now divorced from the absent Emir, and free to do as they wished, but that any soldier who formed a proper union with one of them would receive a grant of land and cash. The Red Army was willing enough, but the ladies of the harem seemed reticent. So Roy issued a further order of the day, permitting the troops to enter the harem and take their pick, *provided* they did so without roughness. He posted himself there to make sure that this provision was not ignored, and described the ensuing selection process:

The storming of the harem took place under strict vigilance, and nothing unpleasant happened. The begums, of course, behaved like scared rabbits, but the sight of the husky young men scrambling for them must have made some impression on them. Able-bodied young men seeking their favour was a new experience to women whose erotic life naturally could not be satisfied by a senile old man. At the end it was a pleasing sight – the secluded females happily allowing themselves to be carried away by proud men.

150

As Vladik and I walked around the monuments of Bukhara, and repeatedly lost our way in its maze of alleys, I wondered if any of the old people we saw had been participants in that epic matchmaking, or were perhaps its fruit. I doubted whether M. N. Roy's breezy account quite coincided with the reality of that day, any more than P. P. Benkov's lurid canvas in Tashkent told the unvarnished truth about the advent of socialism there. Women bred for Islam's purposes in a city whose morals had not budged an inch in thirteen hundred years would probably have behaved like scared rabbits from start to finish of that free-for-all in the harem of the emir's summer palace, where they were taken. The palace had secret stairs leading from the ruler's apartments to the areas where the women were maintained, and overlooking all these places were peepholes so that he could watch his concubines unseen while they rested, while they bathed, while they awaited his command. Not only was he a despot of awful cruelty, but a cunningly surreptitious voyeur.

He was not without taste, though. He had built the palace only a decade before he decamped to Afghanistan, and for all that it jumbled the styles of Asia and Europe more than a purist would applaud, its details were so finely done that they made me smile and brightened a gloomy day. There was a chamber with muqarnas encrusting its alcoves as richly as the honeycombs of the Cartuja outside Granada, and there was an entrance hall ablaze with delicately-coloured patterns on its milky walls that reminded me of the pietra dura adorning the Taj Mahal, except that in Bukhara the effect was created with oil paints and a brush. As with the vitreous tiles that made the religious buildings glow, and the rhythm of the bricks on the Kalan Tower and the mausoleum, these flashes of brilliance provided some relief from Bukhara's darknesses. But not enough for me to understand how the old proverb might have been conceived: 'In all other parts of the world, light descends upon earth. From holy Samarkand and Bukhara it ascends.'

Perhaps in the age of Avicenna and the Samanids, a

reverence for life and for what lies beyond, a celebration of eternity, had suffused this place to the exclusion of all else. If there was such a luminous time it had passed, and too much blood had been wantonly spilt on the edge of the desert here. For all its monumental glories, Bukhara left me unreconciled and ill at ease.

7

Samarkand

For lust of knowing what should not be known,
We take the Golden Road to Samarkand.

Hassan, V, ii

Every journey through Central Asia is a quest for Samarkand. There may not be another place on earth with a sound so peculiarly tempting as this, so laden with remoteness, excitement and an aphrodisiac whiff of danger. Millions who have never strayed far from home have been captivated simply because the idea of Samarkand once attracted Goethe or Marlowe or Milton or Keats, or some other visionary who never saw it either, except through the prism of imagination. The most lustrous tribute of all was composed by a twentieth-century romantic who, for all the distinctly

American cadences of his name, originated in Lewisham and finished up at the other end of an emphatically English spectrum, in Cheltenham. In the course of this progress he never got nearer to his vision than Beirut, where he was for a time a vice-consul, though not a very capable one; possibly because he was rather unhappy so far away from the mutual reassurances of London's literary set. But if he had written nothing else, that one inspired couplet alone would have secured James Elroy Flecker's immortality.

In its latter stages, my own road to Samarkand had brought me through a blizzard of almost impenetrable density. Vladik and I more than once braced ourselves for a crash as our vehicle skidded half-way into a broadside, at which our driver hunched yet more closely round the steering wheel and muttered words of comfort to himself in his Uzbek argot, which was incomprehensible to us. Occasionally the swirling snowflakes would thin out or even lift altogether, long enough for us to see the country we were driving through. It was as bleak as the steppe had been in Kazakhstan, a landscape that sometimes rolled into gentle undulations before settling into flatness again, and all of it looming ominously in the storm. Now and then a settlement could be seen, always some distance from the road, a collection of stone or mud-walled dwellings round which the awful weather howled miserably. But we were not alone in pressing on through this tempestuous whiteness. A battered truck bounced down a rutted track from the highway to a huddle of buildings. We even passed motor-cyclists who were leaning at dangerous-looking angles into the wind in order to keep their balance; and these were the harbingers of our landfall, like birds encountered towards the end of a long voyage at sea.

The blizzard had ceased by the time we were careering down a long and shallow inclination in the land and began driving towards a low range of distant hills. Long before we would have reached them, the Mirror of the World announced itself with a large factory pluming grey smoke into the already heavy sky, and there was further manufac-

154

turing before a modern arterial road gave way to something much narrower and more potholed, bordered by low wooden houses that belonged to the Russian colonisation. Suddenly we were bowling along a wide avenue next to gorgeous antiquities, with trolleybuses humming past us on either side. Coming so soon after that industry on the outskirts, these made it hard to think in terms of a Samarkand that, until the Russians arrived in 1868, was a great deal more remote from the rest of civilisation than the moon is today. Yet, with Bukhara, it was virtually inaccessible once the Silk Route had been superseded by the sea passage to the East; so isolated from the normal traffic of humanity that, in the four hundred years up to 1850, only two Europeans are said to have succeeded in reaching it.

The most ancient of all the antiquities reared above the arterial road just after the factories and before the domiki of the nineteenth-century settlers. This was a brown hillock with fragments of wall on top, and it would have been there when Alexander the Great arrived in 328 BC, when this was Maracanda, chief town of Sogdiana, which approximated to the area later known as Transoxiana, before becoming part of Russian Turkestan and finally Soviet Uzbekistan. To reach Maracanda the Greek army had needed to cross the Oxus, which was wide and deep and flowed as rapidly as the Amu Dar'ya still does today, in the description of Alexander's chronicler Arrian:

Accordingly, Alexander had all the hides collected which served the men for tents, and gave instructions that they should be filled with twigs and other dried rubbish, and then tied up and carefully sewn to make them watertight. When they were filled and sewn, there were enough of them to get the men across in five days.

It was not an auspicious crossing. This large army reached Maracanda in time to hold the annual feast in honour of Dionysius there, though Alexander chose to make his sacrifice to Castor and Pollux, the twin gods who were descended from Zeus himself; a genealogy which Alexander now claimed on his own account. At once there was a dispute within his inner circle of confederates, all of whom that day were drinking heavily, as was their leader. Some began to flatter him by likening him to Hercules, but others deprecated the comparison, believing that it would only further inflate Alexander's already considerable hubris, which made him much less likable than the warrior prince who had first asked them to follow him to the ends of the earth. Among these was one of his oldest friends, Cleitus son of Dropidas, who had saved Alexander's life when it was threatened by a Persian scimitar at the Battle of the Granicus. Drunkenly, Cleitus now ridiculed the idea that Alexander could even be the equal of his father, Philip of Macedon, much less on a footing with Hercules. He said one word too many. Also drunk, Alexander seized a spear and ran him through, and was afterwards filled with a remorse that lasted until his own death five years later in Babylon.

I was to spend a great deal of the next few days wandering round the antiquities of Samarkand, as were scores of tourists, in spite of the fact that this was in the depths of its winter. Not once, though, did I see anyone investigating the remains of Maracanda's outer wall. With the encouragement of their official guides, the visitors were flocking exclusively to the far later monuments, which illuminated the city with walls and pillars and domes clad in vivid tiles much more extensively than the decorations which embellished the religious buildings of Bukhara. They had come especially, of course, to see anything at all associated with the emperor Timur – Christopher Marlowe's Tamburlaine the Great – who chose Samarkand as his capital in 1369. So they tended to make a beeline for the Gur Emir, which he built as a mausoleum for his grandson Muhammad Sultan, and where his own body was interred a couple of years later, in 1405. Then there was the mosque started by his favourite wife, Bibi Khanum, while he was campaigning in India, and in which (according to a totally unsubstantiated legend) he had her walled up on discovering that she had flirted with the architect in his absence. There were also a number of lavish tombs in the necropolis of Shakhi Zinda, on the edge of Samarkand. Otherwise, most of the great monuments were the work of another grandson, Ulugh Beg, or later members of the Timurid dynasty.

Nowhere was more popular than the Registan, which literally means 'sandy place,' where an open market was always held; which is a humdrum way of introducing an extravaganza that moved Lord Curzon to one of his most eloquent testimonies. He thought it nothing less than "the noblest public square in the world," and enlarged on this most generously:

> I know of nothing in the East approaching it in massive simplicity and grandeur; and nothing in Europe, save perhaps on a humbler scale – the Piazza di San Marco at Venice – which can even aspire to enter the competition. No European spectacle indeed can adequately be compared with it, in our inability to point to an open space in any Western city that is commanded on three of its four sides by Gothic cathedrals of the finest order.

It was this phenomenon which caught my eye when Vladik and I drove into town and found ourselves among trolley-buses in the traffic pouring down a side of the Registan.

The other three sides were enclosed by high portals, by arcades and galleries, by solid walls, by domes and by minarets, though not oppressively: every piece in that composition could be enjoyed at a distance, across intervening space. Whatever shape and texture these buildings might have had, that balance between space and substance would have been satisfying enough. The shapes were upright, crossed by strong horizontals, with the roundness of domes a little distance behind; and the relationship between each shape, the substance of the whole, was just enough to maintain the enclosure, to prevent the composition disintegrating into the space. Yet it was not only a triumph of building, but a crowning exhibition of purely decorative art as well.

157

Patterns that were only tentative in Bukhara had reached their full flourish here. Colours which had mingled blithely there achieved even more spectacular harmonies now. Tiles which glistened with light at certain times of day, were even more seductively lambent when the sun had shifted a point or two and transformed their surfaces into matt. Not an inch of any exterior had escaped the genius responsible for illuminating these walls. For all the sumptuous inlay of its semi-precious stones, the Taj Mahal in Agra was made to seem virginal beside the Registan in Samarkand. Nor was this stunning effect confined to what was visible outside. Most marvellous of all the interiors was on the north side of the square, where the seventeenth-century Tillya Kari madrassa and mosque stood. Here was a richness of colour greater than I had ever seen anywhere before, a splendour of red beyond the opulence of rubies and a royal blue of such intensity that it would have hurt the eyes if it had been unrelieved. It was made perfect not only by the alliance with red, but by flashes of orange and dull gleamings of gold which punctuated it and which also emphasised the edge of wall, the curve of arch, the honeycomb of vault, as well as the lozenges, trefoils and other motifs that patterned the topmost smoothness of the dome.

I was enchanted by that chamber, as I was by what lay outside, even though I knew that not one piece of glazed tile, not one fragile sliver of gold leaf, was more than a few years old. The entire decoration of the Registan, some of the building too, was an eye-catching fake to anyone taking an adamantly purist view. One of the minarets on the west side of the square had developed such a tilt after standing for five hundred years that in 1922 it was jacked up to the vertical again, before it came crashing down. That was but a modest intervention compared with the meddling that had followed more recently. Within the past decade or so a new dome had been constructed above the Tillya Kari mosque, to imitate one that had long since collapsed and been scavenged for its materials. Meanwhile, the teams of craftsmen who had settled on the Registan like a cloud of insects were laying fresh bricks to replace shattered ones, reglazing entire frontages with brand new coloured tiles, delicately brushing in the luscious pigments that had me standing beneath that new dome as amazed as Genghiz Khan once was before the Kalan Tower.

To the purist it mattered not that long and painstaking experiment had preceded the bricklaying, the tiling and the application of paint, in order to reproduce exactly the original texture, designs and colourings. That, in a sense, made the offence of the restorers even worse, for not only had they meddled with something whose value was partly its antiquity, in whatever condition it might have survived the passage of time, but they were counterfeiting its originality, which was not theirs to touch. Moreover, the restoration of the Registan was merely the beginning of this pernicious work. Half a mile down the road were the remains of the Bibi Khanum mosque, its tumbled portals standing massively above the adjacent bazaar to give an inkling of its full fifteenth-century magnificence, when it was rivalled in size among all the religious buildings of Christendom only by the cathedral at Milan. A superstructure of scaffolding already encased one of the high archways and a nearby dome, and the derrick of a crane pointed obdurately at the sky above, to signal that the time for restoration had come here, too. And after that, I expect, the dilapidated mausolea at Shakhi Zinda would have their turn, including the grave of Kussam ibn Abbas, who was cousin to the Prophet himself and responsible for bringing Islam to Samarkand, after the Arab conquest, in AD 710. Intent on developing the tourist industry to fortify their feeble economy, the Soviet authorities would not be content until the antiquities of Samarkand had been clad in a meticulous semblance of a pristine past.

And the loss would be great. I could see this well enough, for all that I admired and was charmed by what the restorers had done. There was wonder in the knowledge that a glazed spiral of intricate design in three distinctly different versions of blue, which still clung to the shattered wreck of a Bibi

159

Khanum arch, had been set into the underlying brick by an artisan who almost certainly had seen Tamburlaine the Great ride past: a sense of gratitude as well, because it had managed to hold fast to the wall for five centuries and more, the last remaining fragment of a decoration that would have spiralled dizzyingly in a gigantic ellipse along the full leading edge of the arch. In all the ruins of Samarkand's halcyon days, there was always enough intact for one to see what the original vision must have been. The full power of that buttress could be felt at its base before, higher up, it had crumbled away. The immense sweep of an arch could be told from the way it still sprang from the wall, even though three-quarters of it had vanished in some tremendous collapse. The abstract patterns on these surfaces had nowhere survived without losing many of their pieces, but it was still possible to see how the rhythms must have continued where nothing but pockmarked brick now remained.

And, in spite of the bright colouring that characterised everything built here, the predominantly blue tiling that spelt Islam as much as the domes and the minarets, these dilapidations contained strange reflections of places I had known ever since I was a child. They lacked Graeco-Roman angularity, but they might almost have shared a Gothic pedigree, visible in the curvature of those arches and in those pillars which climbed aspiring into the sky. Walking through Shakhi Zinda and Bibi Khanum, and later venturing south to see what was left of the palace Tamburlaine built at Shahr i Sabz, where he was born, I was reminded most strongly of some English remains. These ruins, notwithstanding the obvious differences, encouraged the imagination to play with them as much as the broken walls at Fountains, at Tintern, at Jervaulx. But pigeons roosted in the mouldering brickwork, instead of the jackdaws and rooks which flew among the stones.

In the end, I came to the conclusion that I was in Samarkand at the best of all times. I side-stepped the argument I had long been familiar with, usually after contemplating the damage done by some crass Victorian to the interior of a medieval church. I didn't think the restorers here had been all that ham-fisted, though inside the Tillya Kari mosque some of the new paint was already peeling from the wall, which the locals blamed on experts from Leningrad who, they said, did not understand well enough the weather in Central Asia. The experts, though, had allowed me to glimpse the full glory of Tamburlaine's Samarkand, even if their achievement was a bit of a spoof. At the same time I could still savour the past in all its precious purity, and enjoy what John Piper once called gently decaying fruitfulness. It seemed unreasonable to ask for more.

That glory, in its original form, marked a difference between Tamburlaine and Genghiz Khan. The Mongol had laid waste to Samarkand in 1220, just after demolishing Bukhara and before going on to do likewise at Otrar and elsewhere. One hundred and fifty years later the city was on the brink of renaissance as Tamburlaine's capital, and throughout his own long career of destruction abroad, Marlowe's "Scourge of God and terror of the world" never failed to send back treasure and skilled craftsmen from his conquests, with one end in view; to make Samarkand worthier than ever of its long renown: not only Mirror of the World, but Garden of Souls and Fourth Paradise as well. He had a creative streak that was lacking in Genghiz Khan or his heirs, whose capital at Karakorum was dismissed as of little consequence by the foreigners who saw it, even though every Mongol campaign also produced artisan slaves who spent the rest of their lives working for the khan at home. And while most of Tamburlaine's creativity was spent on building at Samarkand and Shahr i Sabz, it found at least one other small outlet in the variation of chess he invented, using sixty-four pieces on a board with 110 squares.

In other respects, the two warlords were strikingly alike, and Tamburlaine in fact claimed descent from Genghiz Khan; he was of mixed Turkic-Mongol blood when he was born Timur, son of a provincial governor. Twenty years later

161

came the injury that led to the longer and more familiar form of his name: the arrow through the leg that resulted in a permanent limp and Timur i Leng, Timur the Lame. One source reckoned that he was shot while trying to steal a sheep, another that the wound was acquired honourably in battle; and battles increasingly filled his life from now on. He conducted his warfare with a ferocity that matched Genghiz Khan's own, a record so awful that it impressed itself upon the English playwright a couple of centuries later: "Barbarous and bloody Tamburlaine . . . Bloody and insatiate Tamburlaine!" It was said that after he had sacked Delhi, not even a bird moved there for two full months, a lament that could have been heard wherever he led his armies, which was much more extensively than Genghiz Khan ever took his. The khan had stopped short at the River Indus in his southern progress, but Tamburlaine went far beyond, to devastate not only Delhi but Lahore, and have himself proclaimed Emperor of Hindustan. He was by then sixty years old, yet someone remarked that he was still "strong and robust in body, like a hard rock." Already he had destroyed Baghdad to the west, and had led his soldiers close to Moscow in the north. It was the conquests of Tamburlaine that began the end of the Pax Mongolica. He was marching on China when he died, probably from some pulmonary disorder contracted during a bad winter in the field.

The Timurids who came immediately after him did not have his stomach for butchery. His son Shah Rukh repaired some of Tamburlaine's damage in Persia and established his court at Herat, which attracted painters, musicians, calligraphers, and became especially famous for exquisitely illustrated books. Shah Rukh's own son Ulugh Beg meanwhile sat as his viceroy in Samarkand and developed a talent for mathematics and astronomy, as well as continuing where his grandfather had left off in the construction of beautiful buildings. His most memorable stroke was to establish an observatory on a hill outside the city, whose enormous quadrant may still be examined today. Using this cumbersome apparatus in the first half of the fifteenth century, he calculated the length of the stellar year to within a few seconds of estimates made by the most advanced electronic instruments available at the end of the twentieth. Ulugh Beg became emperor himself in due course, but his short reign ended appallingly. His scientific discoveries, like Galileo's later on, disturbed the religious orthodoxy of his time and he was done to death by Islamic fundamentalists, led by his own son Abd al Latif. There followed several decades of internecine strife between one Timurid prince and another, always to do with power, with pride of place; but a characteristic pattern was taking shape through it all, in the line of descent from Tamburlaine. The brutal aesthete was now a stock character in the dramas of Central Asia, though the greatest days of this heredity would come further south.

From this line emerged the Mughals – which is the word Persians used for Mongols – who were to conquer all but the southernmost tip of India and bequeath, after much bloodshed, marvels of painting and architecture that have been among the subcontinent's greatest treasures ever since. The first of them was Babur, Tamburlaine's great-great-great-grandson, who took Samarkand by force when he was only fourteen but subsequently wrote much elegant verse and composed an autobiography which became one of the classics of oriental literature. In 1526 he won the decisive Battle of Panipat, which left 20,000 Indians dead, and at once celebrated the occasion by planning a garden on the site. Not one Mughal emperor was exempt from such contrary urges. Each in some way was a barbarian, and all had a most sensitive feeling for civilised things, especially in the fine arts. Babur's son Humayan revenged himself upon a treacherous brother by blinding him, but spent most of his time collecting illuminated manuscripts, and came to his own death by falling down the steps of his library. Akbar coldly massacred 40,000 Rajputs after they had impeded his progress a little at Chitor, yet he patronised painters grandly and gave us Fatehpur Sikri, one of the most haunting inspirations in stone to come out of East or West. Jehangir, who was an opium addict and a drunkard, has dissidents impaled on stakes lining a street, but he was an enthusiastic natural historian who enlisted artists to record the flora and fauna of seventeenth-century India in a marvellous collection of paintings. Shah Jehan came to the throne over the bodies of a brother, two nephews and two cousins, all murdered in order to eliminate every possible rival, yet he went on to build the Jami Masjid and the Red Fort in Delhi and, above all, the Taj Mahal. The Mughals who followed these emperors for nearly two hundred years more were in a similar mould, though their barbarities were much restricted from the moment – towards the end of the eighteenth century – aggressive Englishmen with imperial ambitions of their own began to nullify their power.

Samarkand was therefore not only a grail to be enjoyed for itself alone: it was also a source of much that had enthralled me in India for many years. I wandered around its remains with the absorption of a pilgrim who finally sees the relics he has heard about all his life, though no faith was at stake here, to be strengthened or disastrously undermined by scraps of wood or cloth or bone. I was disappointed in only one thing, and that was of the here and now.

I had once seen a painting which depicted a grisly moment in Samarkand's not too distant past.* A great crowd of men were assembled before the Shir Dor madrassa which forms one side of the Registan, and although the building was splendidly decorated it was also mottled by the absence of many tiles which had obviously dropped off the frontage, the minarets and the dome in the course of time. On the sand in front of the portal a dozen tall posts had been driven into the ground, and on each of these was a human head. The crowd was listening to a fellow whose arm waved contemptuously at these trophies of victory by the Uzbeks over invading Russian troops. Some of the spectators sat on camels, others on horses, one upon an ass, but most were

* 'Celebration' by V. V. Vereshchagin (1842–1904). It hangs in the Tretyakov Gallery in Moscow.

164

sitting or standing in the sand. What made the painting bearable in spite of those ghastly heads and the incitement to further atrocity was the exotic counterpoint of the building and the crowd, which was dressed as all Uzbek men would have been until recently, with great individuality. Some wore furry caps with flaps that came over the ears, others sported skin bonnets that rose in a cone. Most wore heavy turbans, yet the yards of cloth had not been wound round every head in a uniform way, but with subtle differences that told of tribal allegiance, family grouping, personal taste. They were dressed in long coats and cloaks, which fitted loosely for greater comfort in the summer heat; and these had been worn vividly in a multitude of designs and different hues. The tackle that each man had at his waist, or attached to his mount, or lying beside him on the ground, also expressed his preferences: knives of different shape, saddlery made by his own hand for his special convenience, water vessels that might be goatskin, leather bottle or canvas bag, depending on his experience, his prejudice, his whim. Everything about these people was not only colourful but emphasised their attractive variety.

When I looked at their descendants in Samarkand now – and the descendants of some who had avoided decapitation after marching down from Russia – it was depressingly clear that although many benefits had doubtless been conferred by the Bolshevik Revolution upon this population, seventy years of communism had turned them into a monotony of drabs. There was no longer any human counterpoint to the exuberant colour of the old buildings. It was a bit unfair to compare a summer painting of the great square with winter along Registanskaya Street, when everyone was muffled against the cold, but I suspected that the seasonal difference in costume was not great nowadays. The vast majority of women were not only encased in dark woollen coats with dull woollen scarves wrapped round their heads, but, underneath, most seemed to be wearing the same dress that I had observed everywhere I had been so far: it came in a couple of different patterns with the same loud gypsy colours that

165

spoke of mass-production for a Central Asian entitlement. The men were just as uniformly garbed, the young ones in a very limited number of clothes that could have been bought off the peg anywhere, the old ones in long quilted coats that belonged, like the gypsy dresses, to some regional quota. A scarf worn like a neckerchief around the waist of some greybeard was as far as individuality now expressed itself, together with the choice of fur or wool in the ushanka, the ubiquitous Russian winter cap whose ear flaps can be tied back over the head. If some specifically Uzbek shape of face or shade of skin were ignored in these people, they might have been plodding through the slush with their shopping bags anywhere in the USSR, including Moscow itself. Or they could have belonged to the small army of tourists that, even at the end of February, was encamped in Samarkand.

Many of these were from other parts of Central Asia, some of them Uzbeks from the hinterland. At the Bibi Khanum one day I watched such a woman in whom at least one of the pre-Bolshevik instincts was still primitively intact. She was no longer a maiden but was still well within the years of motherhood. She entered the courtyard of the mosque with a score of friends and a guide, who stopped them beside a curious stone structure in the middle of the yard. It was a very large lectern on which an enormous version of the Koran would have been placed so that it could be read aloud to a congregation gathered in the open air, by some cleric standing on a balcony above. The guide, I imagine, added the information that, according to the old beliefs, any barren woman who crawled under the lectern, between its numerous legs, would soon conceive. He finished, and led his charges to the doorway of the mosque, and they followed, twinkling a little at what they had been told. All but she, who paused and let the others go on. She did not then crawl under the heavy stones, but she leaned forward and placed her hands on them; then ran her fingers swiftly down the lectern's side in some sort of genuflexion of her own, while she murmured something quietly to herself.

Not much differently dressed from the Soviet citizens were the tourists from other communist lands; the jolly Poles, the noisy East Germans, and the party from Budapest who walked round everything in whispers and with other signs of great respect. All the foreigners, as far as I could tell, had been lodged in the hotel where Vladik and I were staying, which was no better and no worse than any other premises run by Intourist. These were not quite indistinguishable from each other, but if one discounted certain variations in the buildings themselves, the differences were as small as those between one Holiday Inn and another, though on a somewhat different plane. The hotel in Samarkand I would recall later for the posters of Rambo and Madonna which someone had taped to the walls of its coffee shop. And for an individual who stood out from everybody else.

He was a big raw-boned man in middle age, with rosy cheeks and crewcut ginger hair, and a double lameness which caused him to walk flat-footed in very heavy boots. When I first spotted him, he was clumping unevenly towards the lifts from the dining-room, responding to the greeting of several Poles as though he were a hero of theirs, or some eccentric who had become their mascot, enjoying this status and happy to deliver whatever was required of him in that role. He raised in salute the tin mug he was carrying, beamed indulgently and boomed, "Och aye!" I had not expected a Scot with such an impeccable credential as that.

"Is it a Campbell or a MacDonald?" I asked, as I walked past.

"It's neither, but you're getting very warm for a Sassenach," he replied, as he stepped with his Poles into the lift.

He was from the Western Isles, I found out next day, when we shared coffee in the corridor outside the shop, which was far too small for its popularity. He had been brought up on a croft, where his mother distilled hooch to make ends meet after his father had been lost when a fishing boat went down. Sandy called this potion malt whisky, "and I havena' touched a drop in ma life!" He himself became a ship's engineer, first working for the company whose green and

167

scarlet livery – 'MacBrayne for the Highlands, the Highlands for MacBrayne' – had once flanked every ferry sailing between Oban and Stornaway, Portree and Mallaig, as well as most of the buses grinding up the Destitution Road and through the Pass of Glencoe. Later he went deep-sea, in steamers that tramped everywhere, but especially in the Baltic trade. And that was where this great love affair had begun. Not the one with Catriona his wife, who had now passed away; but the one that started even earlier, when he had first sailed to Riga, Tallinn, Leningrad. He had been seduced by everything he saw on that shining northern voyage, and every subsequent trip had confirmed his admiration for the Soviet Union and the struggle of its people to achieve the ideals of 1917.

I assumed he was a communist himself by now, even if he had not started out that way, but he denied this vehemently. "I'm a free thinker," he said, tapping his forehead, "not a politician."

"They've made an awful mess of things, in all sorts of ways, haven't they?"

"Och aye, I'm no denying that. I've seen some terrible things these past thirty years, with ma own eyes." He tapped his face again, lower down. "But that's part of the struggle. That's when you see the incredible energy of these people, still fighting to overcome tremendous obstacles. It's awe-inspiring, man."

Awestruck, he had systematically worked his way round the accessible parts of the Soviet Union year after year, for three decades. He had acquired enough Russian to leave his Intourist groups with impunity, and fended for himself as soon as his party reached a new place, disappearing into the public transport system on an exclusive tour of his own. He gave me the impression that he had not been much interested in the antiquities of Samarkand; that while his Polish friends had been towed round the Registan, the Bibi Khanum and the Gur Emir, Sandy had been investigating the markets, the proletarian housing blocks, possibly those noisome factories as well. His satisfaction as he talked to

168

people in their own tongue, but with a Scots accent that did not compromise with Russian inflexions, could have been no more than a feeling of kinship by now. And no less. For here he had made a home of sorts, a gregarious alternative to the lonely cottage that awaited his return in the Hebrides. Twice a year he came here without fail: once for some such exploration as this, then every summer for a couple of weeks at Sochi on the Black Sea coast.

I asked him if he had ever been anywhere else abroad.

"Och aye, I've been all over. Warsaw, Yugoslavia, Hungary . . . "

In his denial of communism, I saw the guarded instinct of his mother, watching the spirit drip from the copper tube, in defiance of the local distillery and in contravention of the excise laws.

He left the next day, bound for Tashkent, Leningrad and Moscow. I was in the lobby when I saw him emerge from the lift, head and shoulders above his surrounding Poles. His lurching gait brought him close to me, as the party headed for their luggage, stacked by the doors. He caught my eye as he laboured past, and grinned with the pleasure of the company he was in. "Don't forget," he called. "It's the energy that counts." And raised his clenched fist in the old Bolshevik salute.

Before we also left, I slipped away for a last communion with Tamburlaine, Ulugh Beg and the other Timurids who lay in the Gur Emir. The most accessible of all Samarkand's antiquities, this was only just round the corner, in a quiet backwater that had reminded Wilfrid Blunt of an English cathedral close. The mausoleum was encircled by a number of houses with an intervening space, and women regularly emerged from their homes to draw water or wash utensils at a number of pumps standing in this close. On sunny afternoons they sat in groups, leaning against one or other of the houses, enjoying the warmth and the view of the great fluted turquoise dome, and the comings and goings of tourists by the busload. Possibly, too, they ruminated on the sublime definition that tiled the drum of the Gur Emir

169

in a calligraphy of white characters outlined against the honey-coloured brick – God is Immortality.

Tamburlaine and his seven companions lay side by side within a low fence of fretted white marble under that dome, in a gloom that needed much more artificial light to reveal the delicate murals all around and high overhead. The tombstones were of white marble also, with the exception of his, which was a lozenge of black, said to have been the biggest piece of jade in the world when it was lowered over the emperor's body nearly six hundred years ago. It was unfortunately no longer in one piece, and patchings down the side showed where breakage had occurred; more earthquake damage, as like as not. But Tamburlaine was assuredly underneath, as Professor M. M. Gerasimov demonstrated in 1941. In the course of restoration at the Gur Emir, he was given permission to examine closely some of the tombs, and he paid particular attention to two exhumed skeletons. He established that Ulugh Beg had indeed been assassinated as described in the traditional accounts; and that Timur had been crippled by an injury to his right leg.

A legend had always insisted that if the Scourge of God were disturbed in his long sleep, catastrophe would follow. A few hours after Professor Gerasimov uncovered these remains, news came from Moscow that the German panzers had invaded Russia and the Ukraine.

8

Zagorsk

The candles in front of the ikonostasis flamed steadily, and light also glowed from the chandeliers. Without them the church would have been in darkness, for no window broke the richness of paintings that covered the walls and rose indistinctly into the shadows of the roof. The screen itself was a treasury of images that climbed, row upon row, into the upper gloom, each ikon separated from the next by no more than the thickness of a frame. Some had been painted in the fifteenth century by Andrei Rublev himself, who was a monk here until his genius was summoned to decorate the Kremlin churches back in Moscow. But holier even than the saints, the Virgin and Child, and the Christ that he had created for the ikonostasis was the ornate sarcophagus which stood in the angle of the screen and the southern wall. For this contained the remains of the saint who had founded the monastery here at Zagorsk. It was to venerate Sergius, the boyar's son, that a number of monks now leaned against the misericords at the back of the church, silently at prayer; and a crippled old priest slumped nearby in a wheelchair; and several laymen and women stood beneath the chandeliers, repeatedly crossing themselves in the Orthodox fashion from right to left. It was the reason, one supposed, that a nondescript fellow with grey stubble on his cheeks lounged among the monks and quietly munched something out of a newspaper. All had their eyes on the silver sarcophagus, where oil lamps hung inside coloured glass under an elaborate canopy. The chandeliers were silver, too, and so were the candelabra in front of the screen, as well as the thick frames separating one row of ikons from the next. But the candlelight transformed all the silver, so that it appeared to be gold. The church felt curiously warm in that light, although the snow was quite deep outside.

Three young women had ranged themselves one behind the other along the southern wall below the shrine, and the reason for this became clear when a hidden monk began to chant on the other side of the ikonostasis. Quickly the women took it up in voices of almost boyish purity, their heads fractionally turned towards the wall, so that the sound travelled upwards and then across the roof, and seemed to float down on us from above. A young man entered the church and strode straight to the shrine, where he genuflected beside the silver case. Then he fell into line behind the women at the wall and added his voice to theirs.

"My God," whispered Vladik. "Did you see that? The guy actually kissed that grave."

Never before had he been in a church with worshippers, a church that hadn't been reduced to a museum by the state. It was part of his Russian birthright that had totally eluded him till now, deliberately obscured by the distorting processes of the past seventy years. Though he was a son of the high bureaucracy who had received what in the West would have been regarded as an expensive education, he was

172

sometimes ignorant of the national past, and knew it, furiously. In Tashkent one day he asked me what it had been like to be a child of the Second World War in the West, and without thinking to upset him I had mentioned the Soviet–German pact of 1939. He had heard of it but was unaware of its fundamental treachery. He bit his lip and his pale elfin face coloured embarrassingly. I regretted my clumsiness, but he shook off my apology.

"It's not you, it's me," he said. "I don't know my own country's history." He shook his head again, ruefully. "And what I do know I can't trust!"

But he understood some things I was unaware of, and so we filled in gaps in each other's knowledge. I told him everything I knew about Russian expansion into Central Asia in the time of the Tsars and since. He told me that, in accounting for this period, Soviet history books never used the word *zavoyeniye*, which means conquest. Always the Kazakhs, the Kirghiz, the Uzbeks and the others had become part of the empire *dobrovol'noye prisoyedineniye* – by voluntary incorporation. Vladik and I thus became students of his national heritage together. He was pleased when I said I would like to see Zagorsk at last before I flew home. It had always been out of bounds to me before.

We had returned from the South to a Moscow whose mid-winter was depressingly on the way from snow to mucky slush, and the mood of the entire city seemed to have descended in step with the barometer. St Basil's enlivened Red Square with its harlequin domes, and had been generally titivated since my last visit a dozen years before; while some conjurers, pavement artists and other street performers gave the Arbat a certain bohemian vitality that the Soviet capital otherwise conspicuously lacked. I was conscious mostly of people waiting for buses that arrived at each stop already full, of people carrying briefcases and shopping bags as they plodded – they did not hurry and they were never empty-handed – to their destinations because it was quicker that way. They queued for excellent ice cream at a kiosk outside the Belorusskaya Station, and for poor caricatures of hamburger at a mobile stall beside the Intourist Hotel. In shops they queued for anything going, and the one commodity that appeared not to be in short supply was tinned fish. Fruit and vegetables were withered to a stage between the merely inedible and the rank, were much inferior to anything I had seen in the markets of Central Asia, and would not have been countenanced for one moment at home. In the galleried splendour of GUM, which ought to have been as vibrant and as enticing as Istanbul's Great Bazaar, more than half the shops were empty and shut, and most of the rest were scantily stocked. A queue snaked for a hundred yards or more round one of the levels, and when I followed it to its source I found customers emerging with armfuls of loot, having bought three or four of the same thing at once. Men's shirts had just become available and the word had got round.

Misled about the Soviet past, Vladik was also typical of his generation in his response to these manifestations of its present. He was weary of them, impatient with the pace of perestroika. It was through him that I first became aware, with a sense of shock, that unless Gorbachev could solve the Soviet problems with superhuman speed, he might well be deposed by popular acclaim. Bizarrely, I became the leader's apologist, but my companion was not too impressed with Gorbachev's high reputation in the West. Things were not moving fast enough here, in the Soviet Union, and for that Gorbachev was held responsible; only he.

The mess into which they had got themselves was most entertainingly typified in my hotel on Leningradskiy Prospekt, which further enlarged my experience of Muscovite lodgings. On my first visit, twenty years earlier, I had been crammed with hundreds of other foreigners into an hotel which arose monolithically by an inconvenient bend in the river, and where it might easily take half an hour to get from the lobby to a room on the twenty-fifth floor, provided a lift was actually working. My second excursion to Moscow took me to the opposite extreme, when diplomatic hospitality furnished me with an enormous suite on the top floor

174

of the British Embassy, notable for the number of telephones at my disposal, each bearing the conspicuous advice that 'Conversation on this instrument is NOT SECRET.' More memorable still was the view of the Kremlin, directly across the water. Every night I would wake up and spend the next hour or so sitting by the window, enraptured by that floodlit magnificence, whose neon red stars balanced hypnotically on the topmost pinnacles only five hundred yards away. My third appearance saw me installed in a perfect compromise between the earlier alternatives.

My hotel this time was distinctly not for tourists, but for people doing business with the government. It had been built about the turn of the century and Rasputin was said to have disgraced himself here once, though no one could tell me in what way. For the three days of my stay in the capital, in order to confer with Vladik's bosses, I enjoyed an apartment not much less luxurious than my embassy suite, and the public areas were grandiose, with a triumphal staircase as well as much marble and mahogany. The service, alas, did not nearly match these surroundings, though the staff certainly looked the part, as I discovered when I went down to breakfast the first day. The restaurant contained four people when I arrived, and the cutlery before each of them was undisturbed. After five minutes a couple of waiters in tuxedos drifted in and out again without taking an order. There was then a lengthy interval before one reappeared, flourishing his pad as he made for my table. The customers who had arrived ahead of me were still ignored, but I decided this was not the time or the place to be on my best behaviour. Besides, I was hungry.

"*Pozhal'sta,*" I began. "*Est sok e yaishnitza glazuniya e kofye chornya . . . ?*"

He cut me short with a grimace. "*Nye sok,*" he said. "*Mineralnaya voda sevodnya.*"

I declined the offer. I didn't much like soda water before fried eggs. I washed them down with the coffee alone.

Next morning I repeated the order and, this time, without the faintest expression on his face, my waiter brought me

175

about a quart of tinned mango juice in a jug. At first I thought I was being invited to pour myself a small glassful, which was all I wanted. But no, the jugful was all mine. I made myself quite popular with my fellow guests, by passing it round the other tables. I subsequently discovered that this act of largesse cost me £8.

On the third day, dull creature of habit, I again asked for fruit juice, fried eggs and black coffee. My man looked at his watch and said that, as the buffet was not yet open, again there would be no fruit juice this morning. I settled for yoghurt as a preliminary to the eggs. Half an hour later, as I was finishing my coffee, the waiter approached once more and, for the first time in our acquaintance, spoke in English.

"Buffet open now," he said. "How about your fruit water?"

Paul Theroux, after visiting Ulster some years ago, said that every Irish man and woman he met there, both Loyalist and Republican, deplored the daily violence and its causes, but no one accepted the slightest responsibility for any part of it. Always, someone else was to blame. The people here, it seemed to me, were in much the same case. Once, the ills of the Soviet Union were wholly Stalin's fault. Then Brezhnev's. Now Gorbachev's.

The road north-east to Zagorsk swept across a countryside such as Brueghel might have painted, with dark blocks of forest that broke the rolling whiteness of huge fields. It was much like this on all the approaches to Moscow, and my mind's eye populated the landscape with units of the Red Army, desperately fighting to hold the German advance on the capital. Occasionally a village appeared in the lee of a wood, straggling yet compact in these vast surroundings, organically at one with the soil and the trees, yet colourfully painted to stand out against the snow. Smoke whiffled up from every cottage roof, but the only fires had been lit for warmth. Not a ruin, not a charred beam remained as a reminder of times past. For a couple of hours we drove on under the wintry sky. Then the highway dipped into a valley, rose to the crown of a hill, dipped once again and

176

began to climb towards the pretty outskirts of the town, where tall old buildings in pastel shades stood on either side of a narrow main street. To the left and somewhat apart, like a separate township, was the great lavra dedicated to St Sergius and the Trinity.

It looked as immense as the Moscow Kremlin, behind great white and pink battlements which had once withstood a siege for sixteen months. That was at the start of the seventeenth century, when krestianin from the surrounding countryside had joined the monks to repel an army of Poles and Lithuanians, during the well-named Time of Troubles which followed the death of Ivan the Terrible. They were defending, among other things within those walls, the relatively new Uspensky Cathedral whose foundation stone had been laid by Ivan himself, to commemorate his barbaric revenge upon the Muslims at Kazan. Zagorsk had not only become a fountainhead of Christianity from the moment Sergius built his cell and a wooden chapel in the forest clearing in 1345: it was also a very potent symbol of nationality in a land where the religious and the patriotic instincts had for centuries been virtually indistinguishable. When Prince Dmitri Donskoi defeated the Tartars at Kulikovo in 1380 (the first Russian victory over a Mongolian horde in one hundred and forty years) he did so only after making a special journey to receive Sergius's blessing and his approval of the battle plan. Tsars regularly made pilgrimages for a benediction upon momentous enterprises, and a number – including the adolescent who would shortly become Peter the Great – took refuge with the monks in time of danger. Political power may have resided elsewhere; but if there was such a thing as the spiritual heart of Russia it was probably here, in Zagorsk.

In spite of that outer wall which had been built to withstand a siege, and the heavy bastions which marked the four corners of the battlements, the monastery's appearance was not in the least forbidding. There was too much colour, too many incongruously brilliant shapes inside the walls for that, most of them at least partly visible from some distance.

It was a bit like a picture one might expect to find in a book of especially benign fairy tales, an illusion that survived closer scrutiny after entrance through a huge gateway which was decorated with frescoes underneath its arch. The churches and the other buildings which jostled for attention among the trees inside the walls seemed to span the full range of the Russian experience, from the oriental fancy of the onion domes and turrets, by way of the giddiest European rococo, to those sombre Baltic round towers marking the extremities of the lavra. The tallest thing in sight was a campanile that Christopher Wren might have designed, and the most substantial was a palace built to accommodate visiting Tsars, which could just as probably have been the rathaus of an extremely busy municipality somewhere along the Rhine.

The palace was now a theological college, and a number of seminarians as well as resident monks were to be seen striding across the cleared pathways with their cloaks wrapped tightly about them to keep out a cutting wind, and with their black bonnets pulled right down over their ears. A few visitors were around, and most of these did not fail to try the spring water that had caused Sergius to make his profession on this spot. A wonderfully light-hearted chapel had been built over it, a gaily-coloured rotunda that went beyond baroque, with columns twisted like barley sugar sticks beside each window and the door. The water tinkled and plopped from its source under the dome on to a scalloped ledge, where an enamel mug had been placed for those who would drink. Someone had left an empty vodka bottle beside it, the Stolichnaya label still attached. The young monk who sat in a small kiosk, with a rack of tapers for sale, was deep into that day's edition of *Pravda*, oblivious of all else.

A number of his brethren were doing steady business in the vestibule of the Trapeznaya, as worshippers paused at a long counter for candles before going in to attend the liturgy, which was taking place in what had been the refectory of the old monastic establishment. Vladik and I had just come from the Trinity Chapel and its silver sarcophagus, where

178

golden flames gently dissolved into a pervading gloom and everything was indistinct. To step from there into the Trapeznaya was like passing through some fabulous door, which marked a transition from darkness to light, from solemnity to joy. Here, under a long and unbroken curve of barrel vault, was renaissance at its most luminous, fresco at its most dazzling. The paintings began low down each wall, covered the deep window arches and surged across the ceiling in great panels of Christian mythology framed by flights of abstract imagination, by herbaceous borders and by plaster tracery. It was Sistine in its energy, though the only thing much like it I had ever seen before was the Strahov library in Prague, which also tunnelled towards its far wall like this, and was also elliptically decorated. At Strahov, though, there had been a sturdiness imparted by the bookcases lining the walls, and a studious haze seemed to have settled over the room. Here everything was weightless, and everywhere was light. So much illumination came through the windows that the candles and tapers were superfluous, as were the oil lamps in the coloured glass settings of the chandeliers. They were lit, nonetheless, and extra flames were added to this effulgence every time someone else joined the congregation. That was why a number of nuns in dark headscarves and overcoats moved from one candelabrum to another, snuffing out almost spent tapers to make room for ones newly bought.

Beyond the ikonostasis an unseen number of monks, one of the great choirs of Russian Orthodoxy, rumbled and soared through the liturgy; and, listening to them, one could believe that there was need of no other sustenance than this. With less control, with an untempered rawness, the people in the body of the Trapeznaya followed them half a beat behind, women quavering faithfully, men stumbling along doggedly. There was a much greater mixture of people here than there had been in the cathedral congregation at Alma-Ata a couple of months ago. The krestianin might even have been in the minority here, outnumbered by visitors from Moscow and further afield. I watched a young fellow who stood leaning against the padded ledge that ran like an extended misericord the full length of the wall. He was about Vladik's age but unkempt where my companion was daintily neat: he had long uncombed hair and a beard that had not been trimmed for some time. He was singing energetically when he realised that an almost identical figure had entered and was advancing towards him across the tiled floor. He detached himself from the ledge, went to embrace the other, then both took up position by the wall and joined in the singing together. I wondered whether they were Afghantsi who had returned to the faith of their fathers out of simple gratitude. It was said that a number of the vets had done so after surviving an epecially harrowing time against the mujahideen. There may even have been some in the seminary. Perhaps these two were postulants, come to test their vocation in Zagorsk. I was a little wary of the manic gleam in their eyes and the wild gusto of their song, which might one day settle into gentle devotion but now suggested the alarming enthusiasm of the proselyte.

There was one other thing I wanted to see in the lavra before returning to the capital. The Uspensky Cathedral, whose sky-blue domes were dappled with golden stars, which hinted at equally beguiling possibilities inside, was firmly shut; and a monk who emerged from the crypt to feed pigeons as we were passing informed us that shut it would remain until the summer. But outside the west door stood a small structure which itself merited a pilgrimage, though it was of no apparent consequence in these splendid surroundings. It was painted battleship grey, it did not come higher than my chest, and it might well have gone unnoticed by anyone who didn't know what he was looking for. Just below its shallow roof it bore the lettering *Usypal'nitsa Godunovykh*, and there were four very discreet plaques lower down, one for each of its occupants. It was the family vault of the Godunovs, and the notice of its most celebrated incumbent merely said '1605 May 1. The Tsar and Earl Boris Fedorovich of all the Russias.'

So much of Russian history, and of the Russian spirit

interpreted through drama and music, converged in that bleak little shed. Not only the shadow of the cathedral fell over it, but also that of the Uspensky's builder, Ivan the Terrible, who was something more than a ruthless overlord. Like a Mughal emperor in the line of Tamburlaine he was a brute with aesthetic susceptibilities, though his tastes ran to music more than to the other arts. As a youth he had composed stichera for the Orthodox liturgy, and the golden age of Russian singing in its purest national form, just before the old znamenny chant was overtaken by musical innovation from Europe, occurred under the patronage of Ivan and his son, the slow-witted, sensitive Feodor I.* Boris Godunov had been Ivan's protégé and became Feodor's brother-in-law; which meant, in the circumstances of the young Tsar's amiable simplicity, that he was regent in control of state affairs for a decade, until Feodor died heirless and the Rurik dynasty came to an end. A few years earlier Ivan's youngest son, the nine-year-old epileptic Dmitri, who would have succeeded his stepbrother to the throne, had been found with his throat cut, just conceivably though improbably self-inflicted by accident. Yet although Boris Godunov profited from this tragedy when he was elected Tsar – and he was elected, he did not seize power – there was never conclusive evidence that he was an infanticide. He was ambitious and devious, though no more so than any sixteenth-century figure with a chance of great power and, after the rigours of Ivan the Terrible, his reign was a relatively lenient one. Like Ivan, he ruled in alliance with the Church. Not long after becoming Feodor's regent he promoted Metropolitan Job to the superiority of Orthodox Patriarch, the first Russian elevated to that rank. He did not need to lean on anybody for the Church's blessing when his turn came in 1598.

As I walked round that unobtrusive tomb, I asked myself

* Stichera are verses of between eight and twelve lines, invariably on the theme of a given day, often inserted for repetition between the verses of a psalm. Znamenny chant goes back to the end of the eleventh century, but its musical roots are even older, in the melodies of Russian folk songs.

whom we must blame for the caricature of the historical Boris which is presented in the operatic Godunov. Should the fault be laid squarely on the shoulders of Nikolai Karamzin, whose twelve-volume *Istoriya Gosudarstva Rossiiskogo* – which has been described as "a colourful but one-sided account of Russian political history from the 9th to the 16th centuries" – was evidently scrutinised as source material by both Pushkin and Mussorgsky? Was Karamzin just another dilettante whose sloppy scholarship was camouflaged by a diverting gift for imagery and metaphor? Or was it Pushkin's imagination which first turned a suspicion into a certainty, and enlarged on other incidents in order to flesh out the bare bones of the Godunov legend? His own long play, which appeared nearly forty years before Mussorgsky finished the first version of his opera, and on which was based the libretto that the composer wrote himself, portrays Boris starkly as a guilt-ridden child-killer. It also certifies a purely speculative connection between the False Dmitri, who led a successful invasion from Poland on the eve of Boris's death, and the person who may or may not have been the renegade monk Grigori Otryepyev. Pushkin was not obliged to stick scrupulously to historical fact, of course, and perhaps never did. It was he, after all, who gave popular currency to the notion that Salieri poisoned Mozart, with a dramatic poem which Rimsky-Korsakov turned to his own account in a one-act opera.

Pushkin's avowed model when he wrote his own version of the Godunov story was Shakespeare. And anybody familiar with the opera he influenced so much, in whichever of its forms it is presented, cannot fail to be struck by some obvious similarities of characterisation. After the equivocal Shuisky has described the sweet smile on the mutilated face of the dead Tsarevich, and Boris reels around the stage trying to fend off a pursuing spectre (*"Chur, ditya! . . . Chur . . . Chur . . . !"*) we are watching another Macbeth unmanned by Banquo's ghost (*"never shake thy gory locks at me . . . "*). There is a Nurse to comfort a lovesick and grieving Xenia, just as there is a Nurse to humour Juliet through all the tribulations of the romance with Romeo. The scandalous figure of Varlaam, the drink-sodden mendicant working the road for handouts, is none other than a vaguely religious version of that old pisspot Falstaff. He even has a Pistol with him, in the guise of Missail: and the Hostess of the inn on the Lithuanian border is Mistress Quickly to the life, presiding over the Boar's Head in Eastcheap. Shakespeare and Pushkin/Mussorgsky each employ the fool licensed to make sharp points in front of the monarch, whom none other dares offend. The large difference between them is that Feste is the court jester whose primary function is to stimulate laughter, whereas the Simpleton's is a much more serious role. He is that disturbing figure in Russian Orthodoxy who goes back to its origins in Byzantium, the holy 'fool in Christ' who chooses the cross of ultimate humility; for which he is cherished as if he were a child, and heard as if he were a seer. It's said that, as late as 1914, there were no fewer than seven such holy fools in Novgorod, each wearing the hallowed uniform of hairshirt, penal chains and iron cap.

Beyond these coincidences is the particular resemblance between *Boris Godunov* and Shakespeare's histories. There are long passages in this libretto that strike many chords in the Russian psyche, in the same way that speeches by Bolingbroke, Mortimer, Gloucester and King Henry chime with domestic audiences in Stratford-upon-Avon. Varlaam's drunken song in the frontier tavern is a celebration of what Ivan the Terrible did at Kazan, a topic that has already been worked into the previous scene, where it is revealed that Pimen, the Bede figure writing his nation's story in extreme old age, actually took part in the siege as a young man, before becoming a monk. In the scheming Catholic Rangoni and in the Jesuits who turn up with the Pretender's invading army at the end, the Russian opera-goer is reminded of the ever-present threat from the West; and, in the arrogance of Maria, of the specifically Polish bête noire. Like Shakespeare, Mussorgsky expected his audiences to know their past well enough to pick up even the smallest clues, and

183

therefore to remember that the historic figure on whom the Pretender Grigori is based was a servant of the Romanovs before he was Pimen's amanuensis; that his escape from the monastery to Lithuania was assisted by the family that had always rivalled the Godunovs and would, very soon, supply Russia with its last Tsarist dynasty.

Most powerful of all these memories is the one on which *Boris Godunov* totally depends. Except to a few eccentrics, the murder of two young Plantagenet princes in the Tower of London cannot have meant much to the English for several hundred years. But the violent end of the Tsarevich Dmitri has held the Russian imagination without pause ever since 1591. The name of Uglich, where it happened, is a code word of great potency which summons all manner of terrible ghosts. Osip Mandelstam used it in a poem not long before he himself fell victim to tyranny in Stalin's time. In the opera the genie is invoked from the moment Boris first appears, and is never absent for very long. The most terrible invocation of all comes in Act IV. Teased by urchins, the Simpleton is still distraught when the Tsar comes by and asks the holy fool to pray for him. "No Boris, I can't. I mustn't," the Simpleton replies. "I can't pray for Tsar Herod. The Mother of God won't allow it!" There is no comfort for anyone in this Simpleton.

Nor has there been much from any quarter after that first rapture outside the cathedral, in the marvellous procession of boyars and streltsi and Orthodox hierarchs and guards and flunkeys and children of the nobility, when the new Tsar Boris is applauded by the crowd as a long-sought deliverance. Long live our sovereign! Hail, our father Tsar! Honour and glory to you our father! Tsar, our guardian! From this brief exaltation the descent to despondency and suffering is swift, with no tranquillity, no stability for the Tsar or anyone else. Boyars be merciful, Russia is doomed, God ha' mercy, Russia groans, pray God to save Holy Russia! And this is the dominant in *Boris Godunov*. An Italian, a German, a French equivalent of Mussorgsky's opera is unimaginable.

It is set to some of the most highly charged and evocative

music ever heard in an opera house: Mussorgsky's to start with, overlaid more often than not with Rimsky-Korsakov's corrections and embellishments; a bar added here, a key changed there, more vivid orchestration all over the place. Yet what, between them, they have done goes beyond their own skills in composition. They have tapped – and given a separate life of its own in the theatre – the profoundly musical instinct of the Slav; the haunting, primitive and utterly Russian sound made by the human voice and by one almost indigenous instrument; the ringing of church bells in the Orthodox way. This is not the mathematical method of the English campanologists, taking their exercise with rope and wheel, but a tintinnabulation of jangled bells with a clopping of wood for counterpoint, and an ominous booming for requiems and days of reckoning. The bells are heard often in *Boris Godunov*; to celebrate Boris's coronation, to give warning of his funeral, to mark the stages of his way to nemesis. The only sounds more memorable than these are the songs that have been drawn from the very soul of a groaning land.

Standing by that dingy grey wall in Zagorsk, with Godunov's bones lying just on the other side of it, I remembered the first time I saw the opera. Christoff sang Boris and I thought, that night, I had heard nothing more moving in my life than his soliloquy in Act II. It was not the words that affected me, for I understood no more than the drift of Christoff's Russian from the Covent Garden programme notes. What was conveyed to me by that tremendous diapason made translation superfluous. Here was someone close to despair, tortured by memory, longing for peace, wearing himself out, almost done; yet struggling still, with nobility. That was the point: whatever he had done, he had nobility. And all of it communicated by pure sound alone, not by intelligence. The passage moves me still, whenever I hear it, no more and no less than the first time, even though I now know the words almost by heart. Every Boris I have heard produces the same effect, which comes from something richer than individual artistry. And whenever Boris is

185

onstage his tortured power dominates, as does no other character I can think of in any opera I have seen.

Except once. Although everything at the coronation scene is contrived, obviously, to focus attention on the new Tsar, it is nevertheless the chorus which holds the audience, the chorus whose image lingers longest in the mind. Nor is this simply because the décor is sumptuous with copes and mitres, cloaks and baubles, banners and staves framed in a setting of ikons and incense clouds; for nothing, usually, is more compelling than the splendidly costumed presence of Boris Godunov. But when the chorus sings, it is with a majesty to make the heart leap, transcending even the nobility of that prodigiously solo bass. There is no such competition again, which is just as well for a soloist's equanimity when every chorus in the opera seizes the attention like this, though not always majestically. The assembled voices hold us in thrall in whatever role they are cast; as a medley of boyars, citizens, clerics, blind beggars, urchins and functionaries of the court at a moment of rousing pageantry; as a rabble of peasants taunting a boyar and using an old woman cruelly as bait; as a monastic choir which would ease the parting of soul from body with its chant. In everything may be heard traces of old Rus and its musical wealth, in phrases which come from the early notations of the Orthodox and from the folk-singing that excited the Reverend Coxe in 1772; harmonies which always were intermingled even before Modest Mussorgsky was inspired. The choruses are the most memorable part of *Boris Godunov* for me now, for they are Russia itself. They are the reason why, although the original ending at Boris's death has the dramatic force of personal tragedy, the revised version touches me more because it speaks of a greater anguish.

"Tears are flowing," sings the lonely Simpleton: but not for Boris does that thin, high tenor lament. The sorrow is for Russia, for her soul, for her poor starving folk at the last.

Yet, even beside the Godunov vault, I was not conscious of this melancholy during those few hours in Zagorsk. This was partly because of the singing in the Trapeznaya, which had been as grandly operatic as anything the Bolshoi could produce. For years I had wanted to hear that choir in the place where it belonged, rather than disembodied remotely on magnetic tape, and it had left me on a high that would take some time to subside. Nor could I have been glum in surroundings which almost absurdly avoided religious solemnity, with star-spangled domes and Hans Andersen doorways and bulbous shapes on towers that reminded me much less of Russian Orthodoxy than of Ali Baba and the Forty Thieves. So it was lightly that I said goodbye to Boris, before Vladik and I made our way across the lavra's enclosure to the massive gatehouse, with its cheerful murals underneath the arch.

As we began our drive back to Moscow over the Brueghel landscape, I was aware that this was no longer populated only by grim and anguished phantoms from the Great Patriotic War. Now it was possessed by a people of much wider significance, who could be joyful as well as sad, who had triumphed as well as suffered, who could be callous as well as amiable, who were hidden as well as expansive, and who in all their recurring tragedies had not been broken but had endured resiliently until another time for resurrection came. I saw them so in an ageless line down all the years, upon the whiteness of the rolling fields and in the smoky villages sheltered by trees, amidst great forests and along mighty rivers until, more distantly, they crossed the immeasurable flatness of the steppe and sang their hymns of longing and submission against the cold high mountains of the Tien Shan.

And went beyond.

GLOSSARY

---

apparatchiki   functionaries of government, party or trade unions in the Soviet Union. Generally used with contempt by those who are not
aul   settlement/encampment of yurts
bashi   headman/manager of caravanserai etc.
basmatchi   bandit
battue   a form of hunting which involves driving large numbers of animals or birds from cover, so that they can be killed in the open
caravanserai   accommodation at caravan staging post
chai-khana   tea house
domik   traditional style of Russian cottage in wood, which in its simplest peasant form is known as *izba*
harram   Arabic word for whatever is forbidden to Muslims on religious grounds; eg. pork or alcohol
ikonostasis   the elaborate screen which, in an Orthodox church, separates the congregation from the sanctuary where only priests may go. It is always covered with ikons (holy images)
irmos   in the Russian Orthodox liturgy, the theme-song, which

188

varies according to the calendar and other considerations
kathedra   in an Orthodox church, the dais on which the bishop stands
krestianin   peasant. The Russian for Christian is virtually the same, with slightly different pronunciation
kumiss   mildly fermented mare's milk, a traditional drink in Central Asia
kurt   milk curdled into solidity. Another tradition of the steppe, but not recommended
lavra   Orthodox monastery
madrassa   Islamic religious school
maulana   religious dignitary in Islam
muqarnas   a honeycomb pattern of vaulting in classical Islamic architecture
naccara   war drums used by Genghiz Khan's Mongols
nomenklatura   the privileged élite in the Soviet Union
oblast   an administrative region, the Russian equivalent of a French département or English county
Okhrana   Tsarist secret police, predecessor of the Soviet Vecheka, NKVD, OGPU and KGB etc.
orda   Turkic word for military striking roce in Genghiz Khan's time
proskynetarion   a lectern used to support a particularly important ikon
quriltai   assembly of Mongol chiefs
serai   abbreviation of caravanserai
tarantass   a four-wheeled and horse-drawn Russian carriage
transhumance   seasonal movement of sheep over long distances for best pasturing
tumen   a unit of the Mongol army corresponding to a modern division, with 10,000 men
verst   Russian measurement, two thirds of a mile
yurt   traditional tent of Central Asia, dome-shaped, with felt laid over wooden ribs